AutoCAD® Essentials

An Unintimidating Introduction to AutoCAD and AutoCAD LT

Bill Fane

Addison-Wesley Publishing Company
Reading, Massachusetts • Menlo Park, California • New York
Don Mills, Ontario • Wokingham, England • Amsterdam
Bonn • Sydney • Singapore • Tokyo • Madrid • San Juan
Paris • Seoul • Milan • Mexico City • Taipei

Many of the designations used by manufacturers and sellers to distinguish their products are claimed as trademarks. Where those designations appear in this book, and Addison-Wesley was aware of a trademark claim, the designations have been printed in initial capital letters or all capital letters.

The authors and publishers have taken care in preparation of this book, but make no expressed or implied warranty of any kind and assume no responsibility for errors or omissions. No liability is assumed for incidental or consequential damages in connection with or arising out of the use of the information or programs contained herein.

Library of Congress Cataloging-in-Publication Data
Fane, Bill.
     AutoCAD essentials : an unintimidating introduction to AutoCAD and
   AutoCAD LT / Bill Fane.
         p.   cm.
     Includes index.
     ISBN 0-201-40909-7 (pbk.)
         1. Computer graphics. 2. AutoCAD (Computer file) I. Title.
     T385.F36 1995
     620'.0042'02855369—dc20   94-37372
                                                                          CIP

Sponsoring Editor: Kathleen Tibbetts
Project Editor: Sarah Weaver
Production Coordinator: Erin Sweeney
Cover design: Barbara T. Atkinson
Text design: Sonia Hale
Set in 10.5-point Bookman by Vicki Hochstedler

1 2 3 4 5 6 7 8 9 -MA- 9998979695
First printing, July 1995

Addison-Wesley books are available for bulk purchases by corporations, institutions, and other organizations. For more information please contact the Corporate, Government, and Special Sales Department at (800) 238-9682.

To my dear wife Beverley, who still manages to tolerate me after 29 years

Contents

Contents

Contents

Introduction

Until a few years ago, using a computer for design and drafting work involved spending hundreds of thousands of dollars for equipment and undergoing many months of training. The advent of the high-performance personal computer (PC) and suitable software changed all that. It is now possible to set up a computer-aided drafting (CAD) workstation for a few thousand dollars that has more power than a $500,000 mainframe workstation of the mid-1980's.

A great deal of credit for this breakthrough must go to Autodesk, Inc., whose AutoCAD program is by far the most popular CAD software on the market today. In 1984 there were about twenty thousand CAD workstations worldwide; by early 1995, there were over one million registered copies of AutoCAD alone! And this does not include several hundred thousand copies of Autodesk's related AutoSketch and Generic CAD products.

Almost anyone who used to draw on paper now uses AutoCAD. As expected, it is replacing traditional blueprint drawings for architects, engineers, designers, drafters, and others. It is also used to draw electronics schematics and to lay out printed circuit boards. Many governments use it for mapping and keeping track of geographical data.

Unexpectedly, it is also being used in many nontraditional applications; for example, to draw clothing patterns, design theater stage layouts, set up movie special effects and stunt shots, keep track of the furniture in office buildings, design stained-glass windows, and design landscaping, to name a few. It is even being used by the Vancouver Canucks of the National Hockey League to sell hockey tickets.

AutoCAD is an extremely powerful and versatile program, and as such it tends to be complex. It is to Autodesk's credit that the company has also managed to make it very easy to use. By the time you finish this book, you should have a basic understanding of AutoCAD's operation and be able to create and edit your own two-dimensional drawings. You are taken step-by-step through basic principles and into the most commonly used commands. The book concludes with a brief overview of some of the program's more advanced and highly specialized areas, to give you an idea of what else you can do with AutoCAD.

In this book I do not teach you all there is to know about AutoCAD, but rather most of what you *need* to know to get started as a productive AutoCAD operator. This book is not a replacement for all 38 pounds of the full AutoCAD owner's manual set.

I also do *not* cover basic drafting procedures. I am teaching you technique, not style.

1 Getting Started

This chapter briefly reviews the different "flavors" of AutoCAD and their hardware requirements. It then goes on to describe the screen layouts and the basic principles of commands.

AutoCAD Flavors

AutoCAD has evolved into several flavors over the last few years, but they all have a great deal in common. The basic principles this book covers are largely shared by the five most commonly used versions.

▶ *Release 12 for DOS*
  This is the fundamental version of AutoCAD, evolved from the eleven generations of the program running under DOS. It has full three-dimensional capabilities and can be highly customized through several different mechanisms. When it is necessary to differentiate between the versions within this book, this release is called **R12DOS**.

▶ *Release 12 for Windows*
  This release is virtually identical to the DOS version, but it is a Windows application. It has additional features unique to the Windows environment; for example, you can cut out a portion of a drawing and paste it into a word processor document, and you can establish a link between a word processor and AutoCAD so that illustrations in the document are

automatically updated to the latest version in AutoCAD. In this book this version is called **R12Win** for short.

▶ *AutoCAD LT for Windows*
A "lite" version of Release 12 for Windows, this release is basically the same as the full Windows version, except it has very limited three-dimensional and customizing capabilities. Its short name in this book is **LT.**

▶ *Release 13 for DOS*
This is the next generation beyond Release 12. It contains a number of added enhancements and features, but the basic fundamentals remain the same. It is called **R13DOS** in this book.

▶ *Release 13 for Windows*
This is the Windows version of Release 13. It contains the same functional enhancements as R13DOS, and it includes many new user interface features to make its operation more consistent with other Windows applications. It will be identified throughout this book as **R13Win.**

AutoCAD is also available for a variety of other hardware platforms and operating systems, most notably UNIX-based machines and the Apple Macintosh. These versions are relatively rare, but they operate in nearly the same way as the PC versions. It will not generally be necessary to identify them in this book.

In addition, drawings from earlier releases, such as Release 11 for DOS (R11DOS), can be read by any later release. Further, R11DOS can read R12DOS, R12Win, and LT drawings. R13DOS and R13Win can also be made to save a drawing in a file format that can be read by R11, R12DOS, R12Win, and LT, but certain drawing features unique to R13 will be lost. Other than this, earlier releases cannot read newer drawings.

Hardware Requirements

The PC versions require a computer that has the following:

▶ A hard drive with sufficient free space. This may range from about 8 megabytes (MB) to 75 MB depending on the

AutoCAD flavor and on whether all the samples, tutorials, and such are installed.

▶ A 386, 486, or Pentium CPU. The PC versions will *not* run on the older XT or AT (286) machines.

▶ A math coprocessor. A 386 requires a 387 coprocessor. Note that a 486DX or Pentium machine includes the math coprocessor internally; but if your machine has a 486SX CPU you must buy a 487 coprocessor.

▶ A graphics board. AutoCAD can run on older Hercules, CGA, and EGA boards, but a VGA, SVGA, or better board is recommended.

▶ Enough RAM. AutoCAD will run (or, more accurately, crawl) with 2 MB of RAM. There is no such thing as too much RAM; 8 MB is a practical minimum and 16 MB or more is highly recommended, especially for R12Win and R13Win.

▶ An input device. Most people use a mouse or digitizer tablet, but a joystick can also be used with R12DOS.

Also, Windows must run in 386 enhanced mode to run R12Win, LT, and R13Win.

The Macintosh, UNIX, and other versions require specific hardware, which can be obtained from a dealer.

Installing and Starting AutoCAD

To install AutoCAD, you must use the INSTALL program from the first diskette of the full AutoCAD diskette set. R12DOS is installed from the DOS prompt; R12Win and LT must be installed using the Windows File Manager.

R13 is usually shipped on a single diskette plus a CD-ROM (but it is also available on a full set of diskettes—over 40!—instead of the CD-ROM), and is supplied in both DOS and Windows versions. The INSTALL program on the diskette will install R13DOS from the DOS prompt, or the Windows File Manager can run the SETUP program on the diskette, allowing you to install either R13DOS or R13Win, or both. If you install both, they must be installed on a single machine and only one may be run at a time; you cannot legally buy a single package, install R13DOS on one machine and R13Win on another, and then run both at once.

The best way to learn AutoCAD is simply to jump in and try it. It is very difficult to do any really serious damage, so don't be afraid to experiment and explore.

First I want to establish a ground rule. Whenever I ask you to enter something, you must type in that something using the keyboard and then tap the Enter or Return key, which on many keyboards is also marked with a "down and left" arrow. Don't forget to hit Enter or Return! A common dialog between an instructor and a student goes something like this:

Student:	"My machine froze up! I entered the command and nothing is happening!"
Instructor:	"Did you hit Enter?"
Student:	"Oops."

How you start AutoCAD depends on which flavor you are using and how your particular system is set up. The standard methods for starting AutoCAD from a default installation are as follows:

R12DOS: At the DOS prompt, enter ACAD386.

R13DOS: At the DOS prompt, enter ACADR13

R12Win, R13Win, and LT: Start Windows and then use your *left* mouse button to double-click on the AutoCAD icon.

If you are in R12DOS or R13DOS, did you remember to hit Enter? This is the last time I will remind you.

The Drawing Editor Screen

After some gnashing of the disk drive, AutoCAD displays the *Drawing Editor screen* (called the drawing screen for short). This screen contains three sections common to all versions (drawing area, menu bar/status bar/toolbar, and Command prompt), plus two variable sections (screen menu and toolbox). Figure 1-1 shows the R12DOS drawing screen; the R13DOS layout is identical except the words displayed down the right side are different. Figure 1-2 shows the R12Win screen, which closely matches the LT screen. The R13Win screen resembles Figure 1-2, but not as closely; I will cover the specific differences when appropriate.

Drawing Area

This is the big blank area that takes up most of the screen, where you work on your drawing.

Command Prompt

This is the strip along the bottom of the screen. Commands you type echo beside the Command prompt. Also, AutoCAD's requests for further information in response to your commands appear here. There are two firm rules to remember when things go wrong in AutoCAD:

1. If all else fails, read the Command prompt.

2. If all else fails, read the Command prompt.

I know I said the same thing twice, but it is important enough that it is worth repeating.

This area displays three lines of text. As you enter more commands and AutoCAD returns more prompts, the oldest lines scroll up behind your drawing.

> **R13Win**: The Command prompt region is a separate window. It can be resized to show more or fewer lines of text, and it can be dragged to any position on the screen or reduced to an icon, just like any other Windows window.

Menu Bar/Status Bar/Toolbar

These are the bars across the top of the screen (and along the bottom in R13Win). Their formats vary among the different versions (see the upper parts of Figure 1-1 and Figure 1-2), but

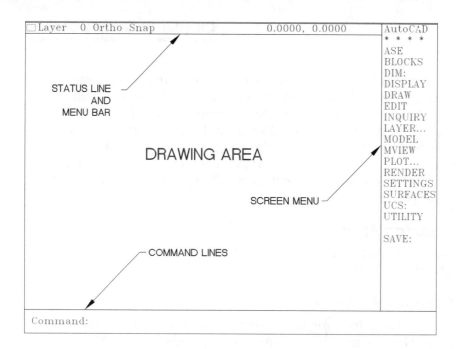

Figure 1-1: The Drawing Editor screen for R12DOS and R13DOS

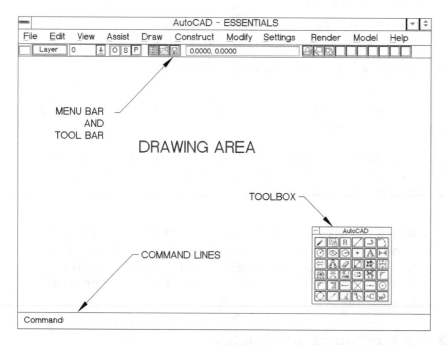

Figure 1-2: The Drawing Editor screen for R12Win, LT, and R13Win

they all operate much the same way. The menu bar provides access to menus containing AutoCAD commands. In R12Win, R13Win, and LT, the menu bar is always visible (see Figure 1-2). In R12DOS and R13DOS it is visible only when you move the cursor up to it (see Figure 1-1).

R12Win and LT include a toolbar containing tool buttons and a status line. The status line keeps track of the status of AutoCAD's operations. The tool buttons activate predefined operations. In R13Win there is a separate status bar, which appears along the bottom of the screen.

Screen Menu (R12DOS and R13DOS Only)

R12DOS and R13DOS provide a screen menu in a column on the right side of the screen (Figure 1-1). You can use this menu to start AutoCAD commands. It largely duplicates the items found in the top menu bar and is a holdover from earlier releases that did not have menu bars. You can turn it off so that you have more drawing area available.

R12Win and R13Win also have screen menus; by default, they are turned off. LT does not have a screen menu.

Toolbox (R12Win and LT)

R12Win and LT include a toolbox of commands, located in the drawing area of the screen (Figure 1-2). You can turn off the toolbox, move it anywhere on the screen, or set it up as a vertical strip down the left or right side of the screen. The toolbar includes a toolbox icon, which when picked changes the location and format of the toolbox. This icon looks like a cluster of six small buttons and is located in the approximate center of the toolbar.

Toolbars (R13Win)

Instead of a full toolbox like in R12Win and LT, R13Win has floating partial toolbars available. These take the form of eleven separate toolbars, each containing ten icons. They can be turned on or off individually, and each can be dragged to any desired location on-screen.

When you first install AutoCAD, only the DRAW and MODIFY toolbars are visible, down the left edge of the screen. You can make a toolbar disappear by clicking on the "minus sign" button in its upper left corner. To make any desired toolbox appear, click on the word TOOLS in the menu bar, then click on TOOL-BARS. This will cause a list of all the toolbars to appear; click on the desired one.

When you exit AutoCAD it "remembers" the toolbar visibilities and locations, so the next time you start AutoCAD it comes back as you left it. As you proceed through this book it may be necessary to click on TOOLS then TOOLBARS then on the desired toolbox because it may not happen to be visible when you want it.

Inputting Commands

AutoCAD provides several different means for entering commands:

▶ Keyboard

▶ Mouse

▶ Menu bar and its pop-down menus

▶ Toolbox and toolbars (Windows versions only)

▶ Screen menu (not available in LT)

▶ Digitizer tablets

Keyboard

You can type in commands directly at the keyboard. Most AutoCAD commands are in plain English: LINE, CIRCLE, ARC, ERASE, MOVE, COPY, and so on. In this book, almost any word that I show in UPPERCASE letters can be entered from the keyboard as an AutoCAD command. In addition, the most common commands can be issued just by entering their first letter; C equals CIRCLE, A equals ARC, L equals LINE, and so on.

After you enter a command, either by typing it in or by using the mouse to pick it from a menu, AutoCAD may request more information. This request appears in the Command prompt area, and it may ask you to indicate a specific point (the start of a line) or a distance (the radius of a circle).

Many commands have alternative actions available; for example, you can define a circle either by specifying the radius or the diameter. A request to specify which alternative to use appears at the Command prompt. When such a request appears, it is necessary to type in only those letters (usually only one) that are shown in uppercase in the request. For example, if you issue the LAYER command you will be asked to specify the desired action: choices include ?/Make/Set/New/ON/OFF/Color/Ltype/ Freeze/Thaw/LOck/Unlock.

Whenever AutoCAD asks for a location, size, distance, spacing, or quantity, you type in the appropriate numeric value.

Of Mice and AutoCAD

The correct way to hold a mouse is to grasp it between your thumb and little finger. Whether you have a two-button or a three-button mouse, you should hold one finger above each button and always use the appropriate finger to press each button. This is faster and more accurate than moving one finger from button to button.

By now you have probably noticed the two lines that cross the drawing screen. These lines are called the cursor, and the point at which they cross is where everything happens. When you move the mouse, the cursor moves. If you run out of desk space before the cursor reaches the edge of your screen, don't worry; simply pick up the mouse, move it over, put it back down, and carry on.

The *left* button is the pick button; when you press and then release this button, actions occur at the point where the cursor lines cross. For example, if you have issued the LINE command, AutoCAD will ask you for a starting point: you can use the mouse to move the cursor to a suitable location, and then press the left mouse button. AutoCAD will start the line from the point where the cursor lines cross.

The *right* button is the Enter button. You may use it at any time instead of hitting the Enter or Return keys on the keyboard.

Some mice have a third button in the middle. Pressing this button causes a menu of "object snap modes" to appear where the cursor happens to be (more on this later).

You can also use the four arrow keys on the keyboard to move the cursor around the drawing screen; but trust me, you normally do not want to use AutoCAD in this way.

The Menu Bar and Pop-down Menus

The menu bar is the list of words across the top of the screen. In R12Win, R13Win, and LT the menu bar is always visible, while in R12DOS and R13DOS the menu bar appears only when you move the cursor to the top of the screen.

To use the menu bar, follow these steps:

1. Move the cursor up to the bar.

2. Pick an item using the pick (left) button on the mouse. A submenu pops down from the selected item. This submenu is called a *pop-down menu.*

3. An item is selected from a pop-down menu by moving the cursor to the word representing the desired operation and then pressing the pick button.

4. Some words have an arrowhead at their right end. Picking one of these items causes another submenu to cascade out from the side of the pop-down menu; some of these may in turn cause a further sub-submenu to cascade out.

5. To get out of a pop-down menu without selecting anything, move the cursor to a blank place on the screen and press the pick button.

To encourage you to use the pop-down menus, I usually give you the names of the menu items, enclosed in braces {}, rather than the formal AutoCAD command name. Because the versions differ slightly, my instructions may not always match letter-for-letter what your computer screen shows, but the intent should be obvious. You may also choose from the Screen menu or the toolbox if you prefer. However, menu picking is usually the fastest way to issue AutoCAD commands; you don't have to take your eyes off the screen or your hand off the mouse. Many experienced users develop the habit of typing in numbers with their nondominant hand rather than moving the dominant one from the mouse. You know, I would give my right arm to be ambidextrous.

The Full Menu in LT

For simplicity's sake, the standard LT menu displays only the most commonly used choices under each pop-down menu. If you want to see all the choices, pick {SETTINGS} and then {FULL MENU}. Picking {SHORT MENU} returns you to the shorter menu. For this book, the short menu is usually adequate, but I will indicate as needed a few significant items that are in the full menu.

Toolbox (R12Win and LT)

The toolbox is the rectangle full of little icons that appears some-where in the drawing area. As you move the crosshair cursor over the toolbox, the cursor turns into an arrow. Move the arrow over an icon in the box, and the name of the command the icon invokes appears in the toolbox header bar. To start running that command, press the pick button.

If the toolbox gets in your way, move the arrow to the toolbox header bar, press and hold the pick button, and drag the toolbox to a more convenient location.

As mentioned earlier in this chapter, you can also change the toolbox location and format by using the toolbox icon, located near the center of the toolbar. This icon looks like a cluster of six small buttons. Click on the icon repeatedly and notice that the toolbox toggles through the following four display modes:

▶ A column down the left edge of the screen

▶ Turned off

▶ A column down the right edge of the screen

▶ "Movable" on-screen

Toolbars (R13Win)

The toolbox in R13Win takes the form of several smaller, "mini" toolboxes called "floating toolbars." The cursor turns into an arrow as you move it into a toolbar. As you move the arrow over each icon, a small text flag called a "tool tip" appears to tell you what each icon does. This is a good thing, because some of the icons are rather cryptic. Icons are great for representing objects, but they do not do so well for concepts.

The individual toolbars can be turned on or off independently, moved to any location on-screen, and arranged as a vertical bar, a horizontal bar, or in several different rectangular patterns.

Many of the icons in the toolbars contain a small triangle in the lower right corner. This indicates that this icon is attached to a "flyout." If you use the mouse to move the cursor arrow to one of these icons and then press and hold the left mouse button, a new set of icons will "fly out" from the one you picked. These usually show several variants of the main icon's command. You can drag the cursor arrow along the flyout to the desired icon, then just release the mouse button to invoke the command.

To help speed up your work, the last selected icon floats to the head of a flyout so it becomes the base icon in the toolbar. When you restart AutoCAD or open a different drawing, the flyouts reset to the default.

The Screen Menu (R12DOS and R13DOS)

The R12DOS and R13DOS screen menu lists AutoCAD commands or can be used to call up submenus of further commands.

To work with the screen menu, do the following:

1. Move the cursor to the edge of the menu. The cursor disappears, and one of the menu's commands is highlighted.

2. Use the mouse to move the highlighting up and down the column of command names until the name you want is highlighted.

3. Pick the name of the command you want to start by pressing the pick button.

    For example, highlight DRAW and press the pick button. In this case, a submenu of drawing commands appears from which you can choose other commands using the methods in steps 2 and 3.

4. Exit the screen menu by moving the arrow cursor to the left, out of the menu. The cursor will reappear.

The word AUTOCAD is always at the top of the menu, no matter which submenus appear. If you get lost in a submenu, picking AUTOCAD will return you to the starting, or root, menu.

Here is a helpful hint that will make it easier to find things in the menus: the contents of most menus are arranged in alphabetical order.

Digitizer Tablets

AutoCAD (except the LT version) also supports most known digitizer tablets. A *digitizer tablet* operates much like a mouse, except it does not roam at random over the desktop. Instead, you move a puck over a special tablet that is energized so that AutoCAD can tell exactly where the puck is, within a few thousandths of an inch. It is called a puck because it is about the size and shape of a hockey puck. It has buttons on it like a mouse, but depending on the brand and model it may have from 3 to 16 or more of them. It also has a clear plastic window in it or attached to its edge. This window contains a crosshair so you can accurately locate the puck on the tablet.

Digitizers can be used when you want to accurately trace an existing paper drawing into AutoCAD. They also can be programmed so that if you move the puck to a predefined location and press the pick button, a command or series of commands will be automatically executed. You can specify dozens of such areas and so can highly automate repetitive drawing operations.

Exiting AutoCAD

To exit AutoCAD, pick {FILE} and then {EXIT}. Read the dialog box and either save or discard your drawing.

One final warning:

DO NOT TURN OFF THE POWER OR REBOOT WHILE AutoCAD STILL SHOWS THE DRAWING SCREEN.

If possible, always exit AutoCAD first before turning off the power or rebooting. If for some reason you can't, the good news is that your current drawing will not be totally lost. AutoCAD regularly performs a safety save to a file called AUTO.SV$. If you do have a disaster you can use the DOS command RENAME to rename this file into something that has the extension .DWG so you can open it in AutoCAD. By default, the interval between saves is 120 minutes, but the SAVETIME command can be used to set it anywhere from 1 minute on up. A setting of zero tells AutoCAD not to do *any* safety saves.

> **R12DOS and R13DOS:** If an accident does occur or your computer freezes, restart your computer and then enter the command CHKDSK /F from the DOS prompt. Depending on how much memory your computer has and how big your current drawing was, CHKDSK may ask you "Convert lost chains to files?" If you are asked this question, type N. You also should use the DOS DEL command to delete AutoCAD's temporary swap files. These files are normally located in the root directory of your hard drive: one has a completely random eight-character name, such as ACBFEBCA, while the other has the same name as the first but with the extension .SWR.

Okay, let's move on to some actual drawing.

2 Entity Creation

An AutoCAD drawing is composed of a number of different entities, the basic objects you use to create your drawing. In this chapter you will learn how to create several of the most common, including lines, circles, and arcs.

Pixels versus Vectors

Before you start drawing, I want to cover two basic principles. These involve how an image is displayed on your computer screen and how the image is stored when it is not being displayed.

An image on a computer screen is made up of "pixels." No, a pixel is not a little sprite like Tinkerbell; a pixel is a "picture element." If you look closely at the screen you will see that the image is formed from a large number of small dots of light, in the same way that newspaper pictures are formed from dots of ink (see Figure 2-1). Yes, I know, Tinkerbell was just a little spot of light too, but this is different.

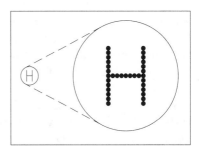

Figure 2-1: Pixels

All computer programs that display a graphic image simply turn on or off appropriate spots to build the picture.

The major difference between *drafting* programs (AutoCAD and others) and *graphics* programs (such as Paintbrush) lies in how they save the image to disk.

When the image from a Paintbrush-type program is saved to disk it is stored as a "pixel map," which lists the color of each pixel. What gets saved to disk is simply a snapshot of what you see on-screen. What you see is all you get.

AutoCAD and other drafting programs also turn pixels on and off to create an image. The difference is that drafting programs work with and store on disk a "vector file." This is a big collection of numbers and words that describe the type, size, and location of every entity in the drawing. When AutoCAD displays your drawing on-screen, it analyzes the vector data and calculates which pixels to turn on or off, depending on which portion of the drawing you are viewing.

You are not limited to working only with what you can see on-screen. You can include as much detail in a drawing as needed. You can zoom in to see more detail and zoom out to see "the big picture." At any one time, the screen displays only those entities and details that the screen is capable of showing. Some screens can show more pixels than others. The number ranges from the 320 per row by 200 rows (320×200) of the old Color Graphics Adapter (CGA) to 1270×1024 and beyond for special-purpose adapters. However, the drawing file always contains the same information. If it were moved to a computer with a higher-resolution graphics adapter, greater detail would show without your having to zoom in as far.

How big is "the big picture"? AutoCAD can draw a circle with a radius of 10^{99} (1 followed by 99 zeros) units, but the known universe is only about 6×10^{22} meters (3.7×10^{19} miles) in diameter. I have a sample drawing, to scale, of the known universe. Not only is it 6×10^{22} meters in diameter, but you can zoom in through the Milky Way to the solar system, the Earth, the moon, a crater on the moon, the lunar lander parked in the crater, and one leg of the lander, until you can read the plaque attached to the leg. The text on the plaque is 3 millimeters (⅛ inch) high.

So it is possible for your drawing file to contain much more than you can see at once. The computer screen is not really the drawing; it is just a viewer that lets you look at all or part of the drawing file.

The Cartesian Coordinate System

Now you need to know how to find your way around in the drawing. AutoCAD uses the Cartesian coordinate system. This means that any location on a drawing can be identified by its horizontal and vertical distance from a starting point, or *origin*. For example, if your address is 625 East 18th Street in a typical town, you live six and one quarter blocks east of First Avenue and eighteen blocks north of Main Street.

AutoCAD uses standard graph notation, in which the origin is at point 0,0, positive values are to the right of and above this point, and negative values are to the left of and below it.

Before you begin drawing, there is a fundamental rule to remember. It takes precedence even over the rules about hitting Enter and reading the command prompt:

DON'T PANIC!

As you wander through the various menu and icon selections, you may inadvertently pick the wrong one or change your mind after starting a command. You can either pick another menu item or icon, which automatically cancels the command in progress, or you can manually cancel it.

> **R12DOS, R12WIN, LT, R13DOS:** Hit the Control (Ctrl) and C keys at the same time, then release them both.
>
> *Note: Two or three keys pressed at the same time to execute a certain function are called a key combination. These will be shown as, for example, Ctrl + C throughout this book.*
>
> **R13Win:** Hit the Escape (Esc) key in the upper left corner of your keyboard.

Note: To avoid excessive clutter, from here on I will not differentiate between R13Win and the other versions; Ctrl + C will mean Escape for R13Win users.

On occasion you may suddenly fall through a crack in the space-time continuum, and your screen will end up in a perpendicular universe that bears no resemblance at all to the AutoCAD drawing screen. Fear not. This is actually fairly normal, and there is an easy way out. What happens and how you handle it depends on your AutoCAD version.

R12DOS, R13DOS: If your drawing suddenly turns to text, hit Ctrl + C and then F1.

R12Win, R13Win, and LT: Two things can happen. First, because of something you inadvertently do, the Help screen suddenly appears and covers much of your drawing. To correct this, move the mouse until the cursor arrow touches the minus-sign button in the upper left corner of the Help screen, and double-click the pick button.

Second, part or all of your drawing screen is suddenly covered by a window full of text. No problem. Just hit Ctrl + C and then F2. (Note that this fix differs from the R12DOS and R13DOS solution to this problem, where you hit F1 instead of F2.)

In this book I will often lay things out in a table. The left column shows what appears at AutoCAD's Command prompt. The right column shows what you enter. The data to enter is displayed in uppercase letters (anything in parentheses is for reference).

Use the Backspace key to delete typing errors. For gross mistakes, you can press Ctrl + C to abort the command and then start over.

The easiest way to understand the concepts of vectors and the Cartesian coordinate system is to jump in and start using the LINE command. First, however, so that you can better see what is happening, turn on AutoCAD's grid of dots. This illustrates the coordinate system.

AutoCAD asks this:	**You do this** (You can type in uppercase or lowercase letters):
Command:	Enter GRID. (Recall that almost anything I show in uppercase letters can be entered from the keyboard as an AutoCAD command.)
Grid spacing (X) or ON/OFF/Snap/Aspect <0>	Enter 1.

Note: Anything AutoCAD displays in angle brackets <> is the default value. To take the default, hit Enter. To use a different value, such as 1, type in the desired value and hit Enter.

Next, hit F7 or Ctrl + G. You should see a pattern of dots all over the screen. The dots are only an aid and are not part of your drawing; they do not show on a plot of the drawing. You can toggle the dots on and off using Ctrl + G or F7 at any time, even while you are in the middle of using another command.

In R13Win you can also double-click on the word GRID in the status bar at the bottom of the screen.

Lines

Leave the grid on and do the following:

AutoCAD asks this:	**You do this:**
Command:	Enter LINE.
From point:	Enter 2,3. (Notice the elastic line that attaches itself to the dot two columns over and three up from the lower left corner of your screen. Move the mouse around and watch what happens.)
To point:	Enter 4,6. (A line appears, extending from the previous dot to the one four columns over and six rows up from the lower left corner of the screen.)
To point:	Enter 5,1.

19

To point: Enter C. (Note how the figure closes back to the starting point. You are then returned to the Command prompt.)

Compare your screen to the drawing in Figure 2-2. Note how the lines connect the dots you specified (see, this is child's play). The numbers in the illustration represent the values you entered. Each end of the line has an *x* coordinate (horizontal location) followed by a *y* coordinate (vertical location). An *x* value and a *y* value together are known as a "coordinate pair." When you enter a coordinate pair, the two numbers must be separated by a comma and cannot contain any spaces.

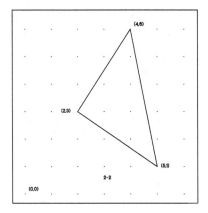

Figure 2-2: Lines and coordinate pairs

Now try a few on your own, picking locations at random. Start LINE again and see what happens when you use coordinates with decimals, such as 1.5,3.5 or 3.625,4.125. What happens if you use negative values, such as –2,–3, in the middle of a sequence? How about bigger values, such as 22,30? Remember, you must always have an *x* coordinate, a comma, and a *y* coordinate before you hit Enter.

When you have finished drawing a series of lines, hit Enter or Ctrl + C to terminate LINE and return to the Command prompt.

Now it is time for your first lesson on how to use AutoCAD more efficiently: if you want to draw more lines, you do not need to retype the LINE command. Just hit Enter or Return or the right mouse button. AutoCAD will repeat the command and let you start another series of lines. In fact, whenever you are at the Command prompt you can just hit Enter to repeat the last command, whatever it was. Here is another tip: the space bar also acts like Enter.

If you entered the coordinate pairs I suggested earlier, then some of your lines will disappear off the edge of the screen. Now enter

ZOOM A and AutoCAD will zoom out to show all of your drawing. This should serve to reemphasize the fact that your drawing is not limited to the area of the screen.

Extents and Limits

Now is a good time to sidetrack a bit and discuss two values that define the size of your drawing: extent and limits.

The extent of a drawing is defined by the coordinate pairs of the lower left and upper right corners of the *smallest* imaginary rectangle that exactly contains everything in the drawing. You have no control over your drawing's extent, except as you add or delete entities. If you add a line that extends farther out than anything previous, your drawing becomes more extensive; if you erase it, your drawing becomes less extensive.

As I said earlier, an AutoCAD drawing can be of unlimited size. This is true; however, big enough paper may not be available to print it. To help you keep your drawings reasonably compact, AutoCAD has the command LIMITS, which enables you to arbitrarily set the coordinates for a suitable lower left corner (usually 0,0) and upper right corner.

Now let's return to the grid. When you turn the grid on, by hitting F7 or Ctrl + G, the dot pattern shows *only to the limits of the drawing*. If you have an entity that exceeds the limits, do a ZOOM All and then toggle the grid on and off using F7 or Ctrl + G. You will see the dot pattern appear and disappear within the limits of your drawing. This can help you determine whether you should either move some of your entities in closer or consider printing on a larger piece of paper.

Generally, AutoCAD works best if the limits are about the same as the extent and if everything is in the positive (upper right) quadrant, where all the *x* and *y* coordinates have positive values.

Earlier I indicated that you are not restricted to drawing within the limits of the screen display. In fact, you exceeded those limits when you entered large numbers for the coordinates in our earlier exercise using LINE. If you are planning a drawing that will exceed the limits, you can set the limits accordingly and then do a ZOOM All. AutoCAD will then zoom out so that the entire drawing area just fills the screen. You can also reset the limits at any time, as the need arises.

Coordinate Displays

It might be nice to know where you are on the screen as you move the cursor. No problem. AutoCAD displays the x and y coordinates of the current active point. Where they are shown depends on the version:

> **R12DOS, R13DOS:** The coordinates are displayed near the right end of the status line, at the top of the screen.
>
> **R12Win and LT:** The coordinates are displayed near the center of the toolbar, at the top of the screen.
>
> **R13Win:** The coordinates are displayed in the lower left corner of the screen.

The numbers displayed in this area can appear in any of three modes. In the first mode, the numbers show the coordinates of the last point picked, such as the start of a line. When you enter a coordinate pair at the keyboard, for example, or pick the end point of the current line segment with the mouse, they show this new point. In the second mode, they roll continuously to show the current cursor position. (The third mode is discussed in the next section.)

Hit F6 or Ctrl + D (for Display) to toggle between these two coordinate display modes.

Coordinate Entries

AutoCAD provides several ways for you to supply coordinate information:

▶ Enter values at the keyboard.

▶ Move the cursor using the keyboard arrows and hit Enter to pick points.

▶ Use the mouse to move the cursor and pick points.

Now you are going to see how AutoCAD also allows several different *formats* for coordinate input.

So far the *x* and *y* values you have typed in have been *absolute* values; that is, they represent total distances from a fixed origin. AutoCAD also allows you to enter *relative* distances; in this case you specify distances relative to the last point (provided there is a last point from which to work).

Falling back on our earlier analogy, if I tell you to go to the corner of 18th Street and Lonsdale Avenue in North Vancouver, I am defining an absolute location; no matter where in the universe you start from, you will end up at the same place. On the other hand, instructions to travel three blocks east and six blocks north will place you *relative* to your current location—where you end up depends on your starting point.

If you have been following every exercise so far, your screen probably looks pretty messy. To clean it up, enter

    ERASE -999,-999 999,999

followed by

    ZOOM A

which will return you to your basic screen display. If the grid dots are not already on, turn them on using F7 or Ctrl + G. Toggle the display by pressing Ctrl + D until the numbers do not change when you move the mouse.

Note: From now on, rather than telling you to type in a command, I will usually give you the menu bar and pop-down menu commands and enclose them in braces {}.

In R13Win most of the common commands from the menu bar and pop-downs have been moved to the toolbars. In most cases the toolbar and button names are close enough to the menu bar headings and pop-down menu items that I do not need to differentiate between them. Braces {} indicate which toolbar to use and the specific buttons to pick. The meaning of most icons is fairly obvious, and as you touch each one with the mouse arrow, a little text flag describing it pops up. And don't forget, the last-used option from a flyout becomes the new base icon.

Next, do the following:

AutoCAD asks this:	You do this:
Command:	**R12DOS or R12Win:** Pick {DRAW} {LINE} {SEGMENTS}. (Pick these three items in sequence from the screen menu or pop-down menus.)
	LT, R13DOS: Pick {DRAW} {LINE}. (Pick these two items in sequence from the menu bar and pop-down menu.)
	R13Win: Pick {DRAW} {LINE} {LINE}. (Use the DRAW toolbar and pick the LINE icon.)
From point:	Enter 1,1 (This is the absolute address from which to start.)
To point:	Enter @1,1. (To enter the @ sign, press and hold Shift and hit the number 2. Then release Shift. AutoCAD uses the @ sign to specify *relative* values. Positive numbers indicate movement up or to the right. Negative numbers indicate movement down or to the left. This entry means, "Go one unit *right* and one unit *up* from the last location.")
To point:	Enter @1,0. (Go one unit *right* and no units *up* or *down*.)
To point:	Enter @0,1. (Go no units *right* or *left* and one unit *up*.)
To point:	Enter @–1,0. (Go one unit *left* and no units *up* or *down*.)
To point:	Enter @0,–1. (Go *no* units *left* or *right* and one unit *down*.)
To point:	Hit Enter. (This terminates LINE.)

You should now have a one-unit square box on your screen with a "tail" going down and to the left, as in Figure 2-3. Even though you entered only 0s and 1s as the coordinates, you got as far as three units away from the lower left corner, because each coordinate value except the first was *relative* to the location just before it.

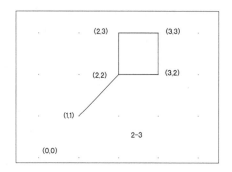

Figure 2-3: Relative coordinates

This feature allows you to quickly and accurately draw an object when you already have fixed dimensions. However, you may well say, "That's great for horizontal and vertical lines, and the 45-degree line I drew by going over one and up one was easy enough, but what do I do with odd angles?"

I'm glad you asked. As ever, AutoCAD has an answer. The answer is polar coordinates, which is just a fancy way of saying, "Give me a length and an angle instead of a coordinate pair."

To supply AutoCAD with polar coordinates, you need to start with the @ sign, followed by the desired length, then a "less-than" symbol or angle (<, which you get by holding down the Shift key and tapping the comma on most keyboards), and finally the value for the angle. Following standard Cartesian practice, angles are measured counterclockwise from "east" or "three o'clock."

Try this example:

AutoCAD asks this:	You do this:
Command:	Hit Enter. (LINE will automatically be repeated because it was the last command you used.)
From point:	Enter 4,4. (This is an absolute location again, just to get started.)
To point:	Enter @1<37.5. (This says to draw a line starting from the last point. It will

	have a length of 1 unit and will be drawn at an angle of 37.5 degrees, measured counterclockwise from the three-o'clock position.)
To point:	Enter @2<–57.3. (Negative angles yield a clockwise direction.)
To point:	Enter @1.5<278. (Large angles, including those greater than 360 degrees, are also allowed. AutoCAD simply keeps on going the specified number of degrees in the required direction.)

Note that I have not instructed you to terminate LINE yet; I first want to show you something else. You have seen AutoCAD display coordinates two ways: fixed at the last point or rolling as you move the cursor. Well, since LINE allows you to supply polar coordinates as well as rectangular ones, you can also have AutoCAD display coordinates in a polar mode. Us F6 or Ctrl + D as a three-way toggle to view the different modes:

▶ Fixed: The display shows the last point selected by the mouse or entered at the keyboard.

▶ Rolling: The display shows the movement of the cursor as it is moved by the keyboard arrows or mouse.

▶ Polar: The display shows a rolling display of the cursor position's distance and angle from the last point.

Watch the coordinate display as you move the mouse around. Press F6 or Ctrl + D and move the mouse some more. Repeat this several times, noting how the display changes as you toggle through the three modes.

If you leave the display in polar mode and then terminate LINE by pressing Enter, the display automatically drops back to an *x-y* mode. Polar mode is not valid at the Command-prompt level because it is a relative mode; until you start LINE and pick the first point, AutoCAD has no starting point from which to be relative. Go ahead and try it. In fact, feel free to experiment with anything at any time, because you cannot do any real damage. Remember, if you get really stuck, Ctrl + C terminates the current command.

More LINE Tricks

Most drawings contain many lines. I have already covered LINE
quite extensively, but there are a couple of additional points I
want to mention.

Not everyone is perfect. Even I make the odd mistake. So
AutoCAD provides an undo facility in LINE.

Try the following:

AutoCAD asks this:	You do this:
Command:	**R12DOS, R12Win:** Pick {DRAW} {LINE} {SEGMENTS}.
	LT, R13DOS: Pick {DRAW} {LINE}.
	R13Win: Pick {DRAW} {LINE} {LINE}.
From point:	Use the mouse and pick any starting point.
To point:	Use the mouse and pick any location for the other end of this line segment. Repeat this step several times, until you have five or six connected lines on-screen.
To point:	Enter U. (Instead of picking a point, enter the letter U, for Undo.)

After you enter U, watch as the last line segment disappears and
the elastic line reattaches itself to the end of the remaining line.
From here you can either pick a new point for the next line segment or enter U again to undo the next previous segment (the
one that came before the segment you just deleted). You can repeat these processes as often as you want and in any sequence.
Go ahead and play. Undo two or three sections, pick points to
add a couple more, undo several, add some on, and so on. If you
undo enough, you end up back at the starting point. Note that
this works only within the *current* run of LINE and while you are

still at "To point." Once you hit Enter or Ctrl + C and return to the Command prompt, entering U undoes the *total run* of LINE.

Another useful feature in LINE is the ability to make a series of line segments automatically close back to the starting point. Try this.

AutoCAD asks this:	You do this:
Command:	Start LINE using your favorite method.
From point:	Pick a start point or enter coordinates. Perhaps you could practice relative and polar coordinates for a while.
To point:	Repeat this step several times to build several line segments. You will need at least two.
To point:	Enter C. (Entering C will make the line close back to the original starting point and terminate LINE.)

Multiple Lines

An advanced form of multiple-line drawing is available to suit special requirements.

R12DOS, R12Win: {DRAW} {LINES} {DOUBLE LINES} starts DLINE, which draws pairs of parallel lines. Their spacing can be varied, and they miter and trim automatically at corners.

LT: {DRAW} {DOUBLE LINES} in the full menu starts DLINE.

R13DOS: {DRAW} {MULTILINE} starts MLINE. This is a more powerful command than DLINE; it defaults to two lines, but it can be customized to include any number of lines and spacings. Lines need not be continuous; you could draw a multilane freeway complete with dotted center lines all in one operation.

R13Win: {DRAW} {POLYLINE} {MULTILINE} starts MLINE.

Figure 2-4 took about ten seconds to draw using a single hit of the double-line function.

This pretty well covers LINE. Now let's move on to create some of AutoCAD's other drawing entities.

Circles

AutoCAD gives you a choice of several different methods for drawing a circle. You can define a circle by specifying

Figure 2-4: Double lines

▶   The center and a radius (the default method).

▶   Three points on the circumference.

▶   Two other entities and a radius. If possible, AutoCAD will draw a circle of the specified radius that is tangent to the other two entities.

In addition, R12DOS, R12Win, R13DOS, and R13Win allow you to specify

▶   the center and the diameter, or

▶   the two points at opposite ends of the diameter.

As always, the best way to learn is to jump right in and try the different methods.

AutoCAD asks this:	You do this:
Command:	From the pop-down menu, pick {DRAW} {CIRCLE} {CENTER, RADIUS}.
. . . <center point>:	Pick a center point with the mouse or type in a coordinate pair.
Radius:	Enter 2.5. (AutoCAD draws a circle of radius 2.5 units, centered on the specified point.)

Command:	Pick {DRAW} {CIRCLE} {CENTER, RADIUS}.
. . . <center point>:	Pick a point to define the center of the circle.
Radius:	Move the mouse and watch as an elastic circle is dragged in and out. When you have a circle of the desired size, press the pick button to freeze it at that size.
Command:	Pick {DRAW} {CIRCLE} {3 POINT}.
First point:	Pick or key in a point.
Second point:	Pick or key in another point.
Third point:	Move the mouse around and watch as AutoCAD draws an elastic circle that passes through three points: the two points you specified plus the moving cursor point. Press the pick button to freeze the circle at a suitable size and terminate the command.

Make sure there are at least two nonparallel lines on your screen. If there aren't, draw them and then try this:

Command:	Pick {DRAW} {CIRCLE} {Tangent, Tangent, Radius}.
First tangent spec:	Use the mouse to pick a line.
Second tangent spec:	Use the mouse to pick another line.
Radius:	Enter a value. If possible, AutoCAD draws a circle of the specified radius that is tangent to the two lines, as shown in Figure 2-5; if not, it asks for another value. You can also "show" AutoCAD the radius by picking any two points with the mouse, typing in two coordinate pairs, or mixing these methods.

Experiment some more. Need you always specify two *lines* in the tangent/ tangent/radius (TTR) mode? What happens if you pick a circle and a line? Two circles? Different points on the circles?

Note that there will probably be more than one possible TTR circle; AutoCAD tries to draw the one that comes closest to the points where you selected the tangent entities with the mouse.

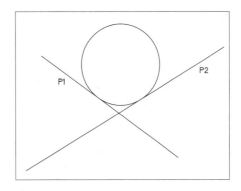

Figure 2-5: Tangent/tangent/radius (TTR)

For R12DOS, R12Win, R13DOS, and R13Win you have two more options:

AutoCAD asks this:	You do this:
Command:	Pick {DRAW} {CIRCLE} {CENTER, DIAMETER}.
. . . <center point>:	Pick or key in a point.
Diameter:	If you move the mouse, AutoCAD will show an elastic circle whose *diameter* is equal to the distance from the center of the circle to the cursor. The elastic circle thus falls halfway between the center and the cursor.
	Enter 2.5. (A circle with a diameter of 2.5 units appears.)
Command:	Pick {DRAW} {CIRCLE} {2 POINT}.
First point:	Pick or key in a point.
Second point:	Move the cursor and watch the elastic circle change. This is the largest circle that will fit between the first point and the cursor; these two locations are the opposite ends of the circle's diameter. Pick a point at which to freeze it.

Arcs

AutoCAD has six or ten different ways to draw an arc, depending on the version. In practice most are useful only for specific applications; most operators usually find it faster to draw a circle and then trim it back to an arc, using the editing commands covered in Chapter 4.

However, there is one very important fact to remember when dealing with arcs: AutoCAD always draws all arcs *counterclockwise*.

AutoCAD asks this:	You do this:
Command:	Pick {DRAW} {ARC} {3 POINT}.
. . . <start point>:	Pick a point.
. . . <second point>:	Pick another point.
End point:	Move the mouse. An elastic arc starts at the first point, passes *counterclockwise* through the second point, and ends at the cursor. Pick a point at which to freeze the arc.

You can experiment with the other methods. Note that not all of them are available in LT, and of those that are, the LT short menu shows only half.

Following is a quick chart of all the ARC options. The letter in the first column refers to the LT menu. F means the option is in the full menu only, while S means it is in both the full and short menus. R12DOS, R12Win, R13DOS, and R13Win support all modes.

S	3 Point
S	Start, Center, End
S	Start, Center, Angle
	Start, Center, Length
F	Start, End, Angle
	Start, End, Radius
	Start, End, Dir

F	Center, Start, End
F	Center, Start, Angle
	Center, Start, Length

ARC also offers the option of drawing an arc that is a continuation of the last line or arc drawn. If you have just drawn an arc or a line, follow these steps:

1. Pick {DRAW} {ARC} {3 POINT}. AutoCAD asks for the "First point."

2. Press the Enter key. AutoCAD attaches the start of an elastic arc to the "youngest," or last-drawn, end of the previous line or arc and asks for the end point.

3. Pick a point or key it in.

A new arc is drawn that is perfectly tangent to the previous entity.

You can repeat these steps as often as desired by hitting Enter twice—once to repeat ARC and once to lock on to the end of the last arc—and then specifying the next ending point. In this way you can draw a series of smoothly flowing arcs that are all perfectly tangent. Note that there is an Arc Continuation item in LT's full menu and R12DOS's screen menu, but all it does is hit Enter twice for you.

In this chapter I have covered the underlying theory of vector drawings and the Cartesian coordinate system. I also covered the LINE, CIRCLE, and ARC commands, which are by far the most used entity-creation commands in AutoCAD.

3 Display Commands

This chapter discusses various commands that let you look at a drawing in different ways. You will not be changing the actual drawing, but only how it appears on-screen.

Chapter 2 explained pixels and the difference between bitmap and vector files. You saw the advantage of a vector file when you drew some lines that disappeared off the screen—you were still able to see them, by issuing a ZOOM All command. You may not have realized the full implications of this at the time, but by the end of this chapter you should be fully conversant with the concept.

An AutoCAD drawing can be of unlimited size. What you see on the screen may be just a small portion of it. Imagine that you are sitting in a chair in front of a small window that looks into the next room. In that room, someone is holding up a paper drawing that is somewhat larger than the window. Because of the relative sizes and positions, you may not be able to see the whole drawing through the small window. So if you want to see a different portion of the drawing, you have to ask the other person to slide the drawing around until the desired portion is visible to you.

Similarly, if you want to see a fine detail in the drawing you will have to ask that it be brought closer to the window. You will be able to see the fine detail in a small portion, but much of the drawing will now be hidden by the wall. Conversely, if you want to see more of the drawing, it will have to be moved further back from the window. Your eyes will not be able to make out the fine detail, but it is still there.

In AutoCAD you are dealing with the same effect. Your monitor screen is analogous to the window cut in the wall. With it you can view part of the drawing in a lot of detail or all of it in less detail. This is illustrated in Figure 3-1. You can also slide the drawing around behind the window to view other portions of it. AutoCAD's ZOOM and PAN commands perform these functions for you.

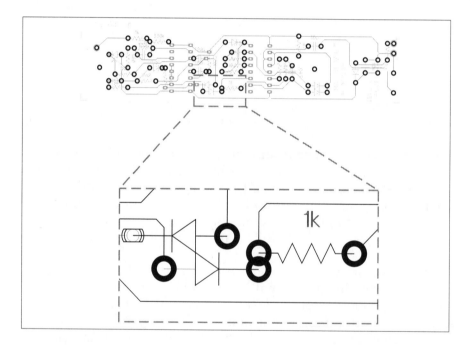

Figure 3-1: Zooming in

The best way to see how these commands work is to bring up one of the sample drawings that comes with AutoCAD. The next section shows you how to bring up, or open, a drawing stored on disk.

Opening a Drawing

1. From the menu bar, pick {FILE} {OPEN}.

   A dialog box appears, and because you have been scribbling through the previous exercises, you are asked if you want to keep or discard your changes. The exact wording of this question and its answer varies some among versions, but the question's intent is obvious.

2. Reply either by moving the cursor (which has turned into an arrow) to the appropriate button in the box and picking it or by entering at the keyboard the *underlined* letter in the label in the desired button. With all due respect for your great artistic talent, you probably want to discard your changes.

3. A new dialog box appears asking you for the name of the drawing you want to open. It displays an alphabetical list of the drawing files in the current directory, plus the names of any subdirectories in the current one. It ignores all other types of files. The layout of the dialog box varies between versions, but the operation is basically the same as the "open a file" dialog box that you find in most Windows applications. You can scroll up and down the list, change directories, and change drives.

   R13DOS and R13Win have an added feature: if you click on the name of a drawing that was previously saved by R13, a window in the dialog box will show you a quick preview of the drawing. You can thus easily find the drawing you want from what can be a list of rather cryptic file names.

   To open the drawing and have it display on-screen, you can either double-click on the desired file name or you can single-click and then pick the "OK" button.

All that having been said, let's see if you can find one of the following drawings. Each version comes with a different set of samples, so I cannot give a standard set of instructions. Assuming AutoCAD is installed on your C drive, open one of the following files:

R12DOS: C:\ACAD\SAMPLE\HOUSEPLN

R12Win: C:\ACADWIN\SAMPLE\HOUSEPLN

R13DOS, R13Win:
C:\ACADR13\COMMON\ SAMPLE\HVAC

LT: C:\ACLTWIN\MOTORCYC

Other drawings also will suffice, but these are particularly suitable for what is discussed next.

ZOOM

Here's looking at you, drawing!

When your selected drawing comes up on screen, follow these steps:

1. From the menu bar, pick {VIEW}.
2. Pick {ZOOM} to bring up the zoom mode choices.

Of the zoom modes available, the following five are the most useful and will account for over 98 percent of your usage:

▶ Window

▶ All

▶ Extents

▶ Previous

▶ Dynamic (R12DOS, R12Win, R13Win) and Aerial View (R12Win, R13Win, LT)

The first four are discussed next, and the fifth under "Avoiding Regens" later in this chapter.

ZOOM Window

ZOOM Window prompts you for one corner of a window. To see how this mode works, follow these steps:

1. From the menu bar and pop-down, pick {VIEW} {ZOOM} {WINDOW}.

2. Use the mouse to move the cursor below and to the left of any region in the drawing that looks interesting, and press the pick button.

   AutoCAD anchors an elastic rectangle at this point and prompts you for another point. As you move the mouse, the window stretches and shrinks to show the area that will be displayed.

3. Move the cursor to display about a 1-inch square window, and pick that point.

   Watch as AutoCAD zooms in, filling the screen with a view of just this one small part of the drawing. As it does, it will probably reveal more detail than was visible when the whole drawing was displayed. (This effect was shown in Figure 3-1.)

4. If you want, pick {VIEW} {ZOOM} {WINDOW} several more times to show ever-smaller portions of the drawing.

Note that the two window points can be anywhere relative to each other; you don't *have* to pick the lower left then the upper right.

ZOOM All

When ZOOM All is selected, AutoCAD zooms out so that *all* of the drawing fills the screen. The result may be loss of detail on a large, complex drawing, but at least you can see where everything is located. ZOOM All displays to the drawing's limits or extent, whichever is larger.

ZOOM Extents

As you might guess, ZOOM Extents zooms out until the total extent of the drawing fills the screen. I lied a little bit when I said that five modes account for 98 percent of your ZOOM usage; ZOOM Extent and ZOOM All are so similar that most operators settle in to using one or the other and hence normally use only four of the modes.

ZOOM Previous

AutoCAD can "remember" the previous view on the screen. Picking ZOOM Previous returns you to that view. To use this mode, follow these steps:

1. Pick {VIEW} {ZOOM} {WINDOW} to zoom in, and then pick it again to zoom in closer.

2. Pick {VIEW} {ZOOM} {PREVIOUS}. AutoCAD returns you to the previous view.

AutoCAD "remembers" the last dozen or so (depending on the version) views; if you have done several zooms, repeatedly picking {VIEW} {ZOOM} {PREVIOUS} takes you back through each view in turn.

Go ahead and practice for a few minutes. What happens if you pick a tall, narrow window? A short, wide one? AutoCAD has to fit everything into the available screen space. It will always show everything in *at least* one direction, and it will show more than you selected in the other direction. If you pick a window that is almost as high or almost as wide as the current view, then the display hardly changes.

Did you notice the quirk in two of the ZOOM modes? Every time you use ZOOM All or ZOOM Extents, AutoCAD takes quite a bit longer to redraw the screen than it does with the other modes. It also displays the message "Regenerating drawing." AutoCAD users refer to this action as a "regen." As your drawings get bigger and more detailed, regens take progressively longer. It sure would be nice to avoid those regens . . .

Avoiding Regens

There are three ways to avoid a regen when you want to see all of your drawing.

ZOOM Previous

ZOOM Previous does not normally cause a regen. Do a ZOOM All to show your entire drawing and wait for it to regen. Now do a ZOOM Window followed by a ZOOM Previous. The ZOOM Previous does not cause a regen, even though it returns your screen to the same display as if you had done a ZOOM All.

ZOOM Dynamic

This command (not available in LT) combines ZOOM All and ZOOM Window into one function. When invoked, it redraws the largest possible view of your drawing (in effect a ZOOM All) while simultaneously allowing you to redefine the zoom window.

ZOOM Dynamic superimposes several marks and rectangles on your drawing. The meanings of these are as follows:

▶ The solid-line white rectangle indicates the total extent of your drawing.

▶ The dotted-line green rectangle indicates the portion of the drawing that was being displayed just before you invoked ZOOM Dynamic.

▶ Four red corner marks, when they appear, mark the previously regenerated area. As long as your selected window area stays within these corners, your drawing will not regen and will zoom in almost instantly. These marks may or may not show, depending on how far you have already zoomed in.

▶ The white rectangle with an X in the center indicates your next view. This box starts out equivalent to the dotted box, but it can be moved and resized using the mouse. Then, when you hit Enter or press the Enter button, AutoCAD zooms in to show the portion surrounded by the box.

To manipulate the X box, press the pick button. The X becomes an arrow pointing at the right edge of the box. You can make the box larger or smaller by moving the mouse left or right; if you move it up or down, the box moves vertically but does not change size.

Press the pick button again. The box's size is locked in. The pick button reverts to allowing you to drag the box around. Press the pick button repeatedly to toggle between dragging and sizing the box.

When the box is the size you want and in the right location, press the Enter button (from either the drag or size mode). AutoCAD zooms in until the portion surrounded by the box fills the screen.

Now for the really cunning parts of the ZOOM Dynamic option. First, as long as the box remains within the red corner marks,

AutoCAD always zooms in without a regen. If you stray outside the marks, AutoCAD displays an hourglass symbol in the lower left corner of your screen to indicate that a regen will be required if you elect to display this portion of your drawing. Often you can display the desired portion of the drawing and avoid a regen simply by moving the box a little.

Second, the box sizing and selection process can occur while AutoCAD continues to generate the drawing in the background. You don't need to wait for AutoCAD to finish displaying the drawing; as soon as you hit Enter, it immediately displays the desired view.

Aerial View (R12Win, R13Win, and LT)

Aerial View mode produces results similar to ZOOM Dynamic and is available only in the Windows applications.

> **R12Win and LT:** Near the right end of the toolbar is an icon that looks like a round compass rose. Click on it.

> **R13Win:** Pick {TOOLS} {AERIAL VIEW}.

AutoCAD now displays the aerial view window—a small window that shows a ZOOM All–view of the drawing. To see how this mode works, follow these steps:

1. Move the cursor into the aerial view window. The cursor turns into a dotted-line cursor.

2. Pick a point with the mouse. The cursor turns into a dotted-line elastic rectangle.

3. Move the mouse and pick another point. AutoCAD quickly zooms in, displaying the region that was surrounded by the dotted elastic rectangle in the aerial view. The dotted-line rectangle turns into a solid-line rectangle. Thus you can always see the whole drawing, plus you know where the current main-screen view is located.

Like any Windows window, the aerial view window can be dragged about by its header bar and resized by dragging its outline border. You can close it by double-clicking on the minus-sign button in its upper left corner or reduce it to an icon on the desktop by clicking on the down-arrow symbol in its upper right corner.

If you have been counting the ways of avoiding regens, you may find that things don't quite add up. That is because ZOOM Dynamic and Aerial View are so similar, and because ZOOM Dynamic is not available in LT, so I only count these two commands as one method. To offset this, there is one more technique to prevent regens, which will be covered later in this chapter under VIEW.

Zoom Scale

Although the five ZOOM modes—All, Window, Extents, Previous, and Dynamic/Aerial View—will account for about 98 percent of your zooming in AutoCAD (especially the last pair), there is one other mode that can be useful. Try the following:

> **R12DOS**, **R12Win**, **and LT:** This mode has no menu pick. You must start the zoom command by entering ZOOM (or just Z) at the Command prompt.
>
> **R13DOS**, **R13Win:** Pick {VIEW} {ZOOM} {SCALE}.

Now enter a ratio in the format of a number followed by the letter *x* (no spaces between parts), such as 2x. AutoCAD selects a point at the center of the screen and magnifies the drawing around it by the specified ratio. This action is analogous to specifying the power of a telescope or binoculars.

You are not restricted to whole numbers, and values less than 1 will zoom out rather than in. This mode is often used to zoom .8x, which zooms back just a little bit to take in a little more area around the edges.

Now that you have mastered ZOOM, it is time to move on to several other display commands.

PAN

Sometimes you might zoom in on a window and then realize you just missed a detail you wanted to get. You could use ZOOM Previous followed by ZOOM Window, but this procedure can be time-consuming on a large, complex drawing. Remember the earlier analogy where I compared your computer screen to a window in a wall with a paper drawing behind it? I said that to see another portion of the drawing it would have to be slid around behind the window. In AutoCAD, PAN lets you slide your drawing around behind your screen so you can see other portions of it. To see how PAN works, follow these steps:

1. Zoom in on part of your drawing.

2. Pick {VIEW} {PAN}. AutoCAD prompts for a "Displacement."

3. Use the mouse to pick a point near the screen's right edge. AutoCAD requests a "Second point."

4. Pick another point about one-quarter of the way across the screen to the left. Notice how the drawing slides over, as though you had reached in through the screen, grabbed the drawing, and moved it.

Try several different pans, including left-to-right and back, up-and-down, and diagonal. What happens if you pick {VIEW} {ZOOM} {PREVIOUS}? AutoCAD pans back to the preceding view. It does not know or care how you got here from the previous view; all it knows is that you want to go back to that view.

VIEW

If you find yourself repeatedly switching back and forth between several parts of the drawing, repeatedly picking the same windows over and over can become a little tedious, even with the convenience of the ZOOM Dynamic or Aerial View mode. There is a simpler way to do this, using VIEW.

VIEW enables you to predefine and then move to specified views of the drawing. Follow these steps to see how this mode works:

1. Pick {DISPLAY} {ZOOM} {ALL} to show the entire drawing.

2. What you do next depends on the version. For LT, pick {VIEW} {VIEW} {WINDOW}. For all other versions, enter VIEW W at the keyboard. All these versions have a series of menu picks, but those picks bring up a bunch of dialog boxes that call up other dialog boxes and so on. It takes about a dozen picks to get to the desired location. I find it faster to enter VIEW W at the keyboard.

3. AutoCAD asks for a View Name. Names in AutoCAD can be up to 31 characters long, but a long name can defeat our objective of simplifying things, so simply enter the number 1.

4. AutoCAD asks you for the two corners of a window. Pick two points at suitable locations. Nothing seems to have happened. Trust me, it has: AutoCAD has remembered the name and the two window corners that you supplied.

5. Repeat the VIEW Window sequence several times for different windows named 2, 3, 4, and so on.

6. From this point, when you want to look at a particular region of the drawing you can restore one of the named views as follows. For LT, pick {VIEW} {VIEW} {RESTORE} and enter one of the numbers you used earlier. For all other versions, enter VIEW R. Once again, there are menu picks but it is faster to type it in.

AutoCAD almost instantly displays the window you picked when you created the named view. This is much faster than doing all that zooming.

View definitions are saved with the drawing, so if you define, for example, views of the plan, elevation, and end elevation of an object or the kitchen, bedroom, bathroom, and so on of a house, they will always be available. Entering a question mark (?) in reply to the VIEW command's main prompt lists all the drawing's current view definitions.

If you add details to the drawing which extend outside a view, simply start the VIEW Window sequence and specify the same name. The new window you specify will supersede the old one.

Having done a series of VIEW Restore sequences, guess what happens if you do a ZOOM Previous?

Important note: ZOOM, PAN, and VIEW do not actually change your drawing; they just alter the way you look at it.

Here is the final trick to avoiding regens. I usually define view number 1 as equal to the entire drawing. The command sequence VIEW R 1 is then equivalent to ZOOM All, without the regen.

REDRAW

Each time you pick an object or the corners of a window, a little blip mark appears on the screen. It is not part of the drawing and serves only to indicate the pick point to you. Eventually the screen develops quite a bad case of the measles. Pick {VIEW} {RE-DRAW}, and AutoCAD will quickly redraw the screen, eliminating all the pick points.

Transparent Commands

The four display commands, ZOOM, PAN, REDRAW, and VIEW, can all be issued while you are in the middle of another command. For example, if you are in the middle of LINE, you can type in the command sequence 'ZOOM W to get a better view of where the line is landing. The apostrophe in front of the command tells AutoCAD to do it "transparently."

When you pick VIEW from the menu bar, most of the display commands are issued in their transparent mode and can be used in the middle of another command. The one exception is ZOOM All, which will always force a regen and so can never be transparent.

Flip Screen

Sometimes you may find yourself wondering just what the heck you did in a previous command. Recall that commands and responses you enter appear beside the Command prompt. As you enter more, the old ones scroll up behind the drawing. AutoCAD "remembers" the last few lines. How to see them depends on the version.

R12DOS, R13DOS: Hit F1. This key is a toggle that turns the drawing display on and off to conceal or reveal the text. You can use it at any time, even in the middle of another command sequence. It shows the last screenful of data (about 24 lines).

R12Win, R13Win, and LT: Hit F2. This key toggles on and off a text screen that has a scroll bar along the right edge. Using the mouse, you can scroll up and down through the last 400 lines. It is a Windows window, so you can also re-size and relocate it so that you can see the drawing and the text at the same time.

Note that these are the same things I told you to do under DON'T PANIC! in Chapter 2.

By now you should be able to find your way around any drawing, no matter how large or detailed it is.

4 Editing

Contrary to what the salesperson told you, you don't really gain a lot of time by doing your basic drawing on a computer. The real power of computer-aided drafting comes when you want to change things or when you want to do something similar to something you have already done. AutoCAD provides a family of editing commands that allow you to move, change, copy, and manipulate an existing entity or set of entities. Unlike the display commands, you now will be changing your drawing.

As you will see, these commands are far faster and more versatile than the traditional paper-pencil-eraser technique. They are not just used for editing, however. They can also greatly speed up the initial production of a drawing.

Selection Sets

First a word about selection sets. To speed things up, AutoCAD allows you to work on any number of entities at the same time. Whenever you issue an editing command, AutoCAD prompts you to select "objects," that is, the entities on which you will operate. You then build a set of selected entities, using several subcommands to add and remove entities until you are happy with the set. When you are done, the editing function is then performed simultaneously on all the entities in the set.

To try this, you need many entities on-screen. The easiest way to achieve this is to pick {FILE} {OPEN} to open an existing drawing. For example, open the one suggested in Chapter 3:

R12DOS: C:\ACAD\SAMPLE\HOUSEPLN

R12Win: C:\ACADWIN\SAMPLE\HOUSEPLN

R13DOS, R13Win: C:\R13\COMMON\ SAMPLE\HVAC

LT: C:\ACLTWIN\MOTORCYC

Remember, when you finish this session, be sure to exit *without* saving any changes or your pretty sample drawing will become mush.

Any editing command can be used to demonstrate the principles of selection sets. ERASE is as good as any to begin with, because it needs no further explanation; its action should be obvious from its name. Follow these steps:

1. Enter ERASE at the keyboard (I will return to the menu pick shortly). AutoCAD asks you to "Select objects."

2. Try either of the following:

    ▶ The cursor is no longer two crossed lines but has turned into a small square. Move the cursor square to an entity and pick it. The entity's appearance changes (on most displays it becomes dotted). A message appears on-screen indicating that a selection has been made. You can continue to pick entities; they will be added to the selection set.

    ▶ Pick an open space on the drawing. Doing this anchors a selection box. AutoCAD then asks for a second corner. What happens next depends on where you pick the second corner.

       If the second corner is *right* of the first, any object that falls *entirely within* the box is added to the set and its appearance changes. Anything that *crosses* or *touches* the box boundary is ignored. This is known as Window mode.

If the second corner is *left* of the first, any entity that *falls within*, *touches*, or *crosses* the box boundary is selected. This is known as Crossing mode.

Figure 4-1 shows the difference between the Window and Crossing modes. The dotted line in the figure represents the selection box. If you were to define this selection box by picking the lower left corner first and then the upper right corner, you would be in Window mode. The circle would be selected, because it falls entirely within the box. The line would not be selected,

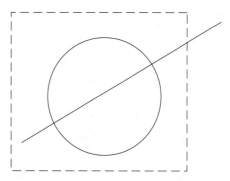

Figure 4-1: Window versus Crossing mode

because it crosses the box boundary. On the other hand, if you were to pick the upper right corner first, followed by the lower left, then you would be in Crossing mode. This would select both the circle *and* the line; the circle because it falls within the box and the line because it crosses the box boundary.

To help you know what is happening, the selection box changes appearance while you are deciding where to locate the second pick point. If the cursor is to the right of the first point, the box outline shows as a solid line to indicate that it will select entities in Window mode if you locate the second pick point there. If the cursor is to the left of the first point, the box outline turns to a dotted line to indicate that it has flipped over and will use Crossing mode if you locate the second point there.

Once you have a suitable set defined, respond to the prompt by hitting Enter rather than selecting anything else. Doing this terminates set selection and executes the command. Because ERASE is currently running, all selected objects will disappear from the screen.

While still selecting entities, you are not limited to just picking them or using a selection box. You can also invoke the following modes by entering the indicated letter or letters when AutoCAD asks you to select entities:

L   The Last entity drawn (the youngest) that is *currently visible* on the screen will be added to the set. Note that this entity is not necessarily the youngest in the entire drawing; younger items that are off-screen are ignored.

R   You can Remove objects from the set by entering an R in response to the prompt. While in Remove, you can point to and remove objects in both Window or Crossing mode. Anything you select is removed from the set and reverts to being displayed normally. Remove remains active until you change mode by entering an A.

A   The Add mode turns off Remove and lets you continue adding items to the set. You can toggle between Add and Remove as desired within one selection process.

P   This mode allows you to add or remove a selection set that was defined for the Previous editing command, whatever it was, without having to select the set again. This obviously does not work if the previous command was ERASE, because the previous entities no longer exist.

ALL ALL selects all the entities in the drawing that are not on frozen layers (more on layers in Chapter 6), even if they are not currently visible on-screen. Entities on all other layers, including Off and Locked ones, are selected.

ALL can also be used to select everything *except* those entities in localized regions of the drawing. Select ALL to select every entity in the drawing, then use Remove to deselect the ones you want to keep. You can thus quickly erase an entire drawing except for a few details that you want to keep.

WP Window Polygon selects objects like Window does, but with one major difference: it does not ask for just two points to define a horizontal/vertical rectangular box. Instead, when you pick the first point it anchors an elastic line. Move the cursor and pick another point. Move the cursor again and you get two elastic lines: one from the initial point and one from the last one. You can carry on picking new points as desired. Each new pick point becomes the new anchor for one of the elastic lines, while the initial point continues to anchor the other one. You can thus draw an irregular polygon around a set of entities.

When you hit Enter instead of picking a point, AutoCAD selects all the entities that fall *completely within* the irregular boundary and adds or removes them to or from the selection set.

CP Crossing Polygon behaves like a Window Polygon except it displays a dotted elastic boundary and selects everything that *crosses* the boundary as well as everything *within* it.

F Fence is a "pure" Crossing mode. You trace out a series of line segments, then hit Enter, whereupon all entities that actually cross the fence are selected. It does not close back on itself like WP or CP and so does not surround an area.

Selection sets are basic to almost every editing command, so practice using these techniques and modes for a few minutes until you are comfortable with selection set creation.

Okay, let's carry on. There are several powerful commands that act on selection sets. All the following commands are found below {MODIFY} in the menu bar unless you are using R13Win, where they are found in the {MODIFY} toolbar.

ERASE

Although ERASE works the same in all versions, the menu set-ups differ slightly.

R12DOS and R12Win: Pick {MODIFY} {ERASE}. A cascading submenu with three more modes, plus OOPS!, appears (OOPS! is covered in the next section):

{Single} erases a single entity or window as soon as it is selected, without allowing you to build a complex selection set.

{Select} allows you to define a complex selection set through the use of the various modes you have already used. The selected entities are erased when you hit Enter instead of making a further selection.

{Last} erases the youngest entity on-screen and immediately returns you to the Command prompt.

R13DOS, R13Win, and LT: Pick {MODIFY} {ERASE}. There is no cascading submenu; instead it defaults to the standard mode, where you can build a complex selection set.

OOPS!

If you suddenly realize you erased the wrong entities, there is a panic button.

R12DOS and R12Win: Pick {MODIFY} {ERASE} {OOPS!}.

LT: Pick {MODIFY} {OOPS!}.

R13DOS: Pick {MODIFY} {OOPS!}.

R13Win: Pick {TOOLS} {TOOLBARS} {MISCELLANEOUS}. This will bring up a toolbar of "miscellaneous" commands; the icon showing the eraser end of a pencil covered by a red circle plus a diagonal line is OOPS!

OOPS! works only for the last set you erased; however, it need not be the next command after the erasure occurred. I find OOPS! to be one of AutoCAD's most valuable commands.

You also can hit Ctrl + C at any time to abort any editing command and return the set of selected entities to their normal display mode, as if you had never even started the command.

MOVE

To use MOVE, follow these steps:

1. Pick {MODIFY} {MOVE}. AutoCAD asks you to "Select objects."

2. Use your selection set mechanisms such as picking, Window, Crossing, Add, Remove, and so on to select a set of entities.

3. When you are finished selecting entities, hit Enter. AutoCAD prompts you to indicate a "Base point or displacement."

4. Enter the coordinate pair 4,0. AutoCAD asks for the "Second point of displacement."

5. Hit Enter. AutoCAD moves the selected entities the indicated horizontal and/or vertical distance as determined by the x and y values of the coordinate pair. In this example, the entities will move 4 units right and zero units vertically, as shown in Figure 4-2.

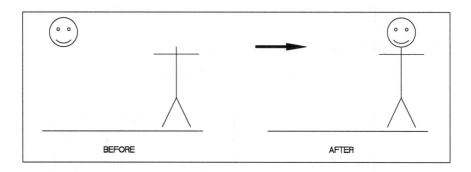

Figure 4-2: MOVE 4,0

Actually, whenever AutoCAD asks for a base point or displacement, you can respond in one of two ways. You have just used the first way: specify an x,y displacement value at the base point or displacement prompt, then hit Enter at the prompt for the second point. This gives a relative distance.

Alternatively, you can respond to the first prompt by moving the cursor to a suitable location and picking a point. At the second prompt, pick another point. You have now "shown" AutoCAD the desired distance and direction for the move. You also can type in two sets of coordinate pairs to define the two points.

Go ahead and practice using both methods of specifying the distance.

Don't forget that hitting Enter at the Command prompt repeats the last command, and you can reply with a P to reselect the Previous set of entities. See what I mean when I said earlier that you can really make money on changes and revisions?

There is only one major caveat regarding MOVE: if you use your mouse to pick the base point for a move and then hit Enter instead of using the mouse to pick the second point, your selected entities will zing off some random distance in a north-northeast direction. Picking {DISPLAY} {ZOOM} {ALL} will show where they went.

BREAK

BREAK partially erases a section of a line, circle, or arc.

AutoCAD asks this:	You do this:
Command:	Pick {MODIFY} {BREAK}.
	In R12DOS and R12Win, you will also need to pick {Select object, 2nd point:}.
	In R13DOS and R13Win, pick {2 POINTS}
Select object:	Pick a line.
Enter second point	Pick a second point on the line and watch the piece in between the points disappear.

Go ahead and experiment:

▶   What happens if you enter F in response to the second prompt? AutoCAD asks you to select the first point again, and then the second. The line will break between the last two picks rather than breaking between the last pick and the point that was used to select the line.

In fact, this is the way BREAK is most commonly used, because often it is not possible to select the line at the same place where you want to break it (for example, with two lines that cross).

▶ In R12DOS and R12Win, what happens if you pick {Select object, Two points:}, and how does this compare to entering F? Answer: the results are the same.

▶ In R13DOS and R13Win, what happens if you pick {Two points, Select}, and how does this compare to entering F? Answer: the results are the same.

▶ What happens if the second point you pick is not on the line? AutoCAD assumes you picked the line anyway, at the location on the line that is closest to the point you actually did pick.

▶ What if the second point is beyond the end of the line? AutoCAD simply cuts the end off the line.

▶ What happens if you BREAK a circle? Remember that AutoCAD always works *counterclockwise* when generating an arc.

▶ What happens if you BREAK an arc? Does the counterclockwise rule apply?

▶ What happens if you type or pick an @ sign in response to the request for a second point? You break out a section of zero length and hence split the object into two pieces that touch at their ends.

▶ In R12DOS and R12Win, what happens if you pick {At selected point}? The same thing.

▶ In R13DOS and R13Win, what happens if you pick {1 point}? The same thing.

EXTEND

Pick {MODIFY} {EXTEND}, pick a line, then hit Enter. Next, pick a line that *aims at* but *does not cross* the first one. What happens? That's right; if you picked the second line close to the end that aims at the first line, the second line will extend until it touches the first.

Try again, but this time when AutoCAD issues the initial prompt, pick several lines before hitting Enter. Now what happens when you pick other lines? I'll give you a hint: if you pick them near an end that aims at any one of the boundary lines, they will extend in that direction until they meet the boundary. If you have another boundary in the opposite direction, you can pick the other end of the line and it will extend that way too.

▶ What happens if you pick an arc or circle as the boundary edge? What happens if you extend an arc?

▶ What if you have picked multiple entities for the boundary edge but later pick one of them to be extended? No problem; if possible, it will extend too.

TRIM

This command is the opposite of EXTEND. The objects you pick *must cross* the selected boundary. They will then be trimmed back. Try some objects, including arcs and circles, and note which parts get trimmed. The results depend on where you picked the object; the portion that you picked gets trimmed off.

Once again you can pick multiple entities to be the boundary edge, and a boundary entity can itself be trimmed if it crosses another boundary.

When selecting entities to be trimmed, you will find the Fence mode particularly useful. You can select your trimming edges and then use Fence to select a bunch of entities to be trimmed; they will all be trimmed at once.

Figure 4-3 shows how easy it is to clean up an intersection.

1. Draw a tic-tac-toe grid of four crossing lines.
2. Select all lines as the trim boundary and use Fence to select them in the center square.
3. Hit Enter.
4. Everything is trimmed back.

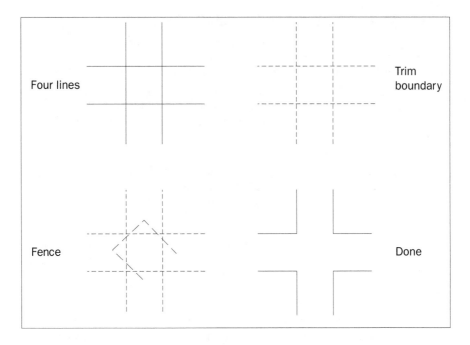

Figure 4-3: Trimming several lines at once

ROTATE

ROTATE allows you to pick a set of entities and rotate them about a specified point (with a name like that, would you really expect it to do anything else?). Let's see if you have learned anything. This time, instead of my giving you detailed instructions on how to rotate entities, I'll just ask you to rotate a set of entities until they are lying on their side. Good luck, and if all else fails, read the prompts. *Hint:* Don't forget that AutoCAD measures angles *counterclockwise.*

STRETCH

Sometimes you draw something and then realize you want to make it bigger in one direction. STRETCH takes care of this by enabling you to move part of a drawing. Unlike MOVE, however, it maintains any connection between the parts you move and the parts that remain.

AutoCAD asks this:	**You do this:**
Command:	Pick {MODIFY} {STRETCH}.
Select objects using the Crossing window:	Select a window by picking two points so that the second is to the left of the first and the dotted elastic window crosses several entities. Then hit Enter.
Base point:	Pick a point.
Second point:	Pick a point above the first point and watch things grow by the distance between the two picks.
	You can make things stretch by a specified amount by entering 0,0 for the first point and an *x* and *y* coordinate pair to indicate the desired stretch distance.

Observe how STRETCH works: the ends of any selected arcs or lines outside the window do not move, while those inside move by the specified amount.

You can try to use the standard selection options, but only those items that cross the *last* window selected will be stretched; anything else will just move. Also, Fence is not a window, so it won't work with STRETCH.

Although this command is called STRETCH, it will also shrink entities, depending on the relative location of the second point. It will also stretch *and* shrink simultaneously: a door can be slid back and forth along a wall and the lines of the wall will stretch and shrink on either side to maintain the connection with the door frame.

The next series of editing commands are found in two different locations, depending on your AutoCAD version:

    R12DOS, R12Win, LT, and R13DOS: Pick {CONSTRUCT} from the menu bar.

    R13Win: Pick the command you want from the MODIFY toolbar flyouts.

COPY

COPY uses the same procedure for selecting entities as do most other editing commands. Like MOVE, it accepts the same two methods of specifying the direction and distance from the original at which the copy will appear. Go ahead and make several copies at different locations. Note that COPY retains the original in the old location, while MOVE erases the original after copying it to the new location.

OFFSET

OFFSET is similar to COPY, except that it copies an object a specified distance away from the first.

1. Start OFFSET.
2. AutoCAD will ask for an offset distance. You can either key in a value or show AutoCAD the distance by picking two points with your mouse.
3. AutoCAD will ask you to pick an entity.
4. Finally, you will be asked to pick a point to show AutoCAD on which side you want the copy to appear.
5. The offset copy appears.

OFFSET allows only one entity to be offset at a time. However, it loops back, allowing you to pick another object to be offset by the same distance.

This command differs from COPY in one other significant way. When used on a circle or arc, it draws a new one using the same center as the first but with a radius that is larger or smaller by the offset amount. It thus allows you to draw two or more arcs or circles that are perfectly concentric.

Go ahead and try it. Draw a line and a circle, then draw offset entities that are .25 unit to either side of them. Try offsetting to either side of the line and both inside and outside the circle.

MIRROR

With MIRROR, you can make a mirrored copy of a set of entities or flip them over. Try both methods.

Start MIRROR.

AutoCAD asks this:	You do this:
Select entities:	Enter P (to select the previous set). Note that the previous set is still valid, even though you are in a different command from that in which it was specified.
Select entities:	Hit Enter (to complete the selection process).
First point of mirror line:	Use the mouse to pick a suitable point.
Second point:	Pick a point to the *left* of the first.
Delete old objects <N>:	Enter N. *Do not* delete the old objects. You will end up with a mirrored copy of the entities, and the originals remain. (Actually, N is the default and need not be keyed in; just hit Enter in response to the prompt.)

Try this again, but this time do it a little differently as follows:

Command:	Hit Enter P Enter. (That is, hit Enter to repeat the last command, then hit P to select the previous set, then Enter again to conclude entity selection.)
First point of mirror line:	Use the mouse to pick a suitable point.
Second point:	Pick a point *above* the first.
Delete old objects <N>:	Enter Y. (You will end up with a "flipped-over" set of entities; the originals disappear.)

You can mirror any line at any angle, not just a horizontal or vertical line.

ARRAY

No, this is not a cheer, as in "hip, hip, array!" ARRAY enables you to build circular or rectangular repetitions of an entity or set of entities. You can choose either a rectangular or a polar array.

Let's say you need a whole parking lot full of individual parking stalls or a circle of bolt holes on a flange.

AutoCAD asks this:	You do this:
Command:	Pick {ARRAY}.
Select objects:	Select several entities in the usual fashion, then hit Enter.
Rectangular/Polar (R/P)	Enter R (for a rectangular array).
Number of rows (---)<1>	Enter 5.
Number of columns (|||)<1>	Enter 10.
Unit cell or distance between rows:	Enter 4.
Distance between columns:	Enter 2.

The result is an array of 50 sets of entities neatly arranged in five rows spaced four units apart, with each row containing ten copies of the selected entities spaced two units apart. You will probably have to pick {DISPLAY} {ZOOM} {ALL} to see them all.

Note the use of AutoCAD's standard convention for indicating direction: you entered positive values, so the array spread out up and to the right from the first one. If you had entered negative values, the array would have gone down and to the left. What happens if you enter one negative and one positive value? Right:

the array grows up and to the left, or down and to the right, as appropriate.

Further, in the example you gave AutoCAD actual numbers for the row and column spacing. However, you can also point to the desired distance and direction by picking two points with the mouse. The array will grow in the direction and with the spacing specified, from the first pick point to the second one. Try it.

One other point that beginners often overlook: when you indicate to AutoCAD the number of rows and columns, you must include the existing item. (In the example, you ended up with a *total* of five rows, not five *more* rows.)

The rectangular array can be used for such actions as laying out a grid of .100-centered holes on a printed circuit board or for setting up 20-foot column spacings in a building.

The other choice under ARRAY is a polar, or circular, array.

AutoCAD asks:	You do this:
Command:	Pick {ARRAY}
Select objects:	Select sets as usual and then hit Enter.
Rectangular/Polar (R/P)	Enter P (for a polar, or circular, array).
Center point of array:	Pick or type in a point.
Number of items:	Enter 10.
Angle to fill (+=CCW, −=CW)<360>	Hit Enter. (Take the default of 360 degrees.)
Rotate objects as they are copied?	Enter Y. (Take the default of Yes.)

The result is 10 sets of entities in a circle, all facing inward. If you had replied N to the last prompt, all the entities would have stayed facing the same way up as they were copied.

A polar array is very handy for drawing such things as a circle of bolt holes on a flange. Be sure to note the "Angle to fill" prompt;

it is not necessary to fill a complete circle. The indicated number of items will be spaced evenly within the specified angle.

FILLET and CHAMFER

FILLET and CHAMFER are not a law firm; they modify what happens where two entities meet. Let's start with FILLET. Make sure you have several nonparallel lines on your drawing, some of which cross and some of which don't, then try the following.

AutoCAD asks this:	**You do this:**
Command:	Pick {FILLET}.
Polyline/Radius/ <select two objects>	Enter R. (This tells AutoCAD that you want to define a radius for the fillet.)
Enter fillet radius <0.000>:	Enter .5. (This will put a fillet with a radius of half a unit where the lines meet. AutoCAD returns you to the Command prompt.)
Command:	Hit Enter. (This repeats the FILLET command.)
Polyline/Radius/ <select two objects>	Pick two nonparallel lines that cross, and watch what happens: AutoCAD will draw an arc with radius .5 that is tangent to the two lines. It will then trim back the ends of the two lines until they meet the ends of the arc.

Next, hit Enter to repeat the command, but this time pick two lines that *don't* cross. AutoCAD will extend the lines if necessary to make them meet the ends of the arc. Note that you get the same fillet radius as in the previous exercise; its value will remain current until you change it by entering R and specifying a new value at the first prompt. You can also specify the radius by picking two points; AutoCAD will take the distance between them as the radius value.

Now try filleting two arcs and/or circles and putting a fillet between an arc and a line. What happens if you specify a radius of zero and then fillet two intersecting lines? Two nonintersecting lines? A fillet with radius zero can be very useful for ensuring that two lines exactly meet at their ends (in fact, that's the default).

Figure 4-4 shows how to steer the location of the fillet. AutoCAD draws the fillet between the two places where you selected the entities. For example, if you selected point P1 at the other end of its line, then you would end up with a "less than" symbol (<) with a fillet at the intersection.

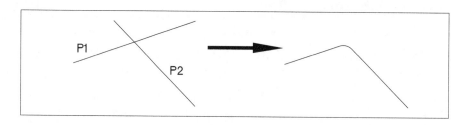

Figure 4-4: Steering a fillet

CHAMFER works much like FILLET, except it draws a straight line at an angle between the two specified lines.

AutoCAD asks this:	**You do this:**
Command:	Pick {CHAMFER}.
Polyline/Distance/ <select first line>	Enter D. (This defines the distance.)
Enter first chamfer distance <0.000>	Enter .5.
Enter second chamfer distance <0.500>	Enter .25. (The default for the second value is the first value. Here, you enter a different one.)
Command:	Hit Enter. (This repeats the command.)
Polyline/Distance/ <select first line>:	Pick a line that crosses another.
Select second line:	Pick the line crossed by the first.

Notice what happens: AutoCAD trims the first line back from the intersection point by the first distance, then trims the second line back by the second distance. Finally, it draws a line from the end of the first line to the end of the second.

Repeat this exercise, but pick the two lines in the opposite sequence and note the difference in the chamfer that is produced. Now try it with two lines that don't intersect; AutoCAD extends them until they do intersect and then chamfers them back.

There is one final point to notice about FILLET and CHAMFER: There is no such *entity* as a fillet or a chamfer. AutoCAD simply draws the appropriate arc or line. Once AutoCAD completes the command, it does not know if the arc or line was produced by FILLET or CHAMFER. You cannot edit a fillet or a chamfer; you must manually erase the arc or line and then run FILLET or CHAMFER again with the new value or values.

Grips

GRIP is not a separate command, but rather a different way to edit. Grips are "handles," in the shape of small boxes that appear on an entity when it is selected under certain conditions. Using grips you can edit entities, including stretching multiple new lines, rubber-stamping multiple moves, and mirroring several copies around different mirror lines. Grips can affect one entity or many. You can also use grips to build selection sets.

To see how grips work, let's look at an example. Follow these steps:

1. Ensure that you are back at the Command prompt.

2. Instead of starting a command, pick a line in your drawing. The line becomes highlighted (dotted), indicating it has been selected. Three small blue boxes appear on the line: one at each end and one in the middle. These boxes are the grips. The blue color indicates they are *warm*, or inactive.

3. You can do nothing with a warm grip; it first must be made *hot*, or active. Move the crosshair cursor until the pick box

at its center is directly over the grip at one end of the line, and then pick the grip.

The blue (warm) grip turns red. A red grip is a hot grip, available for you to use in editing.

Notice that the Command prompt now shows STRETCH. Whenever you are working with grips, AutoCAD displays the command you are using at the command prompt. By hitting Enter or the space bar or pressing the Enter button on your mouse, you can scroll through editing commands until you reach the one you want. Available editing commands, in the order in which you scroll through them, are STRETCH, MOVE, ROTATE, SCALE, and MIRROR (but not COPY, as I will explain shortly).

4. Scroll through the list of commands until you are back at STRETCH. Now simply move the cursor and pick a new location. The line automatically stretches or shrinks so that the gripped end of the line is at the new location.

    Note that the end that moves will be the exact end of the line, regardless of where along the line's length you pick.

At the end of a grip edit function, you are returned to the command prompt. The selected entities remain selected, and the grips remain visible. The hot (red) grip reverts to warm (blue). To edit the selected entities, you need only pick a grip to make it hot.

To deselect the entities but leave the grips visible, hit Ctrl + C. This again clears the grips; that is, it causes them to disappear (become "cold").

Grips are located exactly at the ends and middle of lines and arcs and at the center and four quadrature (compass) points of circles. If you pick the grip on another entity as the target point of an operation, then the operation that occurs will end *exactly* at the picked grip point of the target entity.

COPY is not on the list of available commands, because you can make multiple copies from within any of the other commands. To access COPY, hold down Shift while you are selecting the first destination point. As long as you are holding down Shift you can "rubber-stamp" multiple copies of the parent entity.

If you do not like holding down Shift you can enter a letter C to make multiple copies.

While making multiple copies within a "grip" command, you can enter a letter U to "undo" the last copy. This can be repeated as often as desired to step backwards without exiting the command.

Building Selection Sets with Grips

So far I have implied that you are doing all grip editing on a single entity. However, you also can build selection sets using grip editing. While you are still at the command prompt and before you pick a grip to make it hot, you can continue selecting entities by picking them or by using the Window or Crossing modes. Window and Crossing are automatic; that is, as with other methods of building selection sets, if you pick one entity, it is selected. However, if you pick a random point, AutoCAD automatically starts a window or crossing selection, depending on whether the next pick is to the right or left of the first.

After you select the desired entities, pick one grip to make it hot, and then scroll through the command list as usual. With any command but STRETCH, when you select the target point for the operation, *all* selected entities are acted upon.

STRETCH acts only on the last entity you selected (the one with the hot grip), unless you pick multiple grips. To pick multiple grips, hold down Shift as you pick grips. Each grip you pick becomes hot. However, to actually perform the stretch you must release Shift and then pick another grip. That grip becomes the base grip for stretching *all* the entities that have hot grips.

To remove entities from the set, hold down Shift while picking or windowing or crossing. The highlighting disappears, but the grips remain visible and can still be used for editing.

Hitting Ctrl + C will unselect the entities but leave their grips warm; hitting Ctrl + C a second time will clear the grips.

UNDO

AutoCAD is so clever that it actually has a built-in time machine. That's right: having edited the daylights out of your drawing, you can step backward through time and UNDO each command in turn.

You saw two earlier hints of this; one in the previous section on grips, and one in Chapter 2 in the section on LINE. In addition, AutoCAD has a general UNDO facility that will take you backward through any drawing or editing you have done.

Unfortunately, UNDO is not in the menus of every version, and it is not handled the same in those that do include it in their menus. For purposes of this discussion, it's easier for you to type in the command at the Command prompt.

Enter the single letter U and AutoCAD will undo the last command. Remember that hitting Enter repeats the last command (which is now UNDO) so you can hit Enter as often as you want to back up as far as desired, right back to the start of the current editing session.

Enter the full word UNDO and AutoCAD returns a prompt that offers several options. Many are a little esoteric, but two are particularly useful:

▶   Mark. This leaves a "marker flag" at this point in time, and you can go on to draw or edit all you want.

▶   Back. This returns you to the "marker flag," all in one hit.

Mark and Back need not be used as a pair; you can leave a mark every few commands and then back up to each one in turn.

REDO

What if you undo too far back? REDO undoes the last undo, but only once; that is, you can step backward ten steps, but then forward only one step.

Doo-Doo

This is not an AutoCAD command; it is what you say when you realize that you used UNDO or U twice too often and can only REDO one of them.

This chapter covered how to use the major AutoCAD editing commands. As you have seen, they are far faster and more versatile than manually correcting a paper-and-pencil drawing.

The editing commands can also be used to speed up the creation of the initial drawing itself. For example, you *could* draw an ornate escutcheon plate for an entrance-door handle in about the same time using AutoCAD as you could with paper and pencil. But with AutoCAD it is only necessary to draw one-quarter of it; you could then create the other three quarters in a matter of seconds by using MIRROR twice.

5 Drawing Aids

Drawing aids are commands, settings, and keystrokes that help you produce better drawings and/or speed things up.

> **R12DOS**, **R12Win**, **LT:** Pick {SETTINGS} {DRAWING AIDS}.

> **R13Win**, **R13DOS:** Pick {OPTIONS} {DRAWING AIDS}.

A dialog box appears that lists all the drawing aids, their current values (as applicable), and their current status. This box operates transparently, so it can be brought up at any time, even in the middle of another command. Thus you can change settings "on the fly."

Each aid can be turned ON or OFF. Three of them also require that values be entered. To change a value, follow these steps:

1. Use the mouse to move the cursor arrow to the desired box.

2. Click the pick button. (If you move the highlighting to a specific character before you click, your editing will start at that character.)

   The default is to insert new characters at the highlighting, but you can also delete the highlighted character or backspace over the character to the left of the highlighting.

3. If you want to edit another value, repeat steps 1 and 2.

The *x* and *y* values for each aid can be set to be different from each other, but there is a trick to doing this: when you set *x*, both *x* and *y* change, but if you set *y* first, only *y* changes. So if you want them to be different, you must set *y* after you set *x*.

Clicking on the ON/OFF square toggles between the two states. An X in the box indicates an aid is currently on.

You can change any or all the settings as often as you want. The changes do not take effect until you pick OK in the lower left corner of the main box, after which the dialog box disappears and you are returned to your drawing. Picking CANCEL rather than OK cancels all changes entered and returns the values to their previous settings.

Now let's see what each aid does, starting with one we have already seen, GRID.

GRID

As we saw in Chapter 2, GRID displays dots all over the screen, spaced at a specified distance from each other. I emphasize again that the grid is purely a drawing aid that appears on-screen and *not* on your actual plotted drawing.

If you were doing printed-circuit designs, you might let one drawing unit equal 1 inch and set a grid at .100 units, to show the standard .100-inch spacing grid. An architect might let one drawing unit be 1 inch and set a 12.000-inch grid, to display dots every foot.

If all you want to do is turn the grid on or off, you do not need to bring up the dialog box; simply hit F7 or Ctrl + G, even in the middle of another command.

When the grid is on, it shows the dot pattern only to the limits of the drawing. If an entity goes beyond the limits and you do a ZOOM All, then as you toggle the grid on and off with F7 or Ctrl + G the dot pattern appears and disappears within the limits of your drawing. This can be helpful in determining whether you should move some entities in closer or consider using a larger piece of paper for plotting.

SNAP

Use SNAP when "close enough is good enough" (note that this applies to dancing and hand grenades as well as to AutoCAD). AutoCAD normally measures to 14 decimal places, but you can force it to round off all your pick points to some specific degree of precision.

At first it may seem less accurate to work using only 3 or 4 decimal places instead of 14, but actually it is *more* accurate. For example, if SNAP is on and set to 1.0, you can use your mouse to pick only points whose coordinates are *exactly* 1.0, 2.0, and so on. If you were to pick the same points with SNAP off, you would probably get values like 1.00029356, 1.99927542, and so on.

Try this:

1. Bring up the {DRAWING AIDS} dialog box.
2. Set the SNAP *x* and *y* spacing to 1.0.
3. Turn SNAP on.
4. Pick OK, and you are returned to your drawing.
5. Make sure the coordinate display is on (hit F6 if necessary) and move the mouse around.

Note the action of the cursor and the coordinate display as you move the mouse. The cursor doesn't move for a moment, then it snaps exactly to the next whole-number position. It is impossible to make it go to a location partway between the whole values.

Typical SNAP values might be 0.001 for mechanical design, 0.100 for printed circuit-board layout, ⅛ inch (0.125) for architectural work, and 1 kilometer for cartography.

Note that SNAP is independent of the grid settings; for example, you could have a grid at 1.0 units but a snap of 0.1 units. They need not even be exact multiples of each other.

SNAP increments do not need to be horizontal and vertical. The Snap Angle setting in the dialog box will rotate everything, including the cursor lines and the grid, accordingly. Similarly, the origin does not have to be 0,0 but can be offset as desired; for example, you could have a one-unit snap increment that would always land halfway between the integer values. This can be most useful. If one wing of a building is to be built at a 37-degree angle to another, you could draw the first wing, rotate the SNAP by 37 degrees and move its origin to one corner of the angled wing, and draw the second wing without having to worry about compensating for the angle.

SNAP increments, angles, and origin offsets apply to almost every AutoCAD command, including drawing commands such as LINE, CIRCLE, and ARC and editing commands such as STRETCH, MIRROR, MOVE, COPY, and ARRAY.

As with GRID, you do not need to bring up the dialog box just to turn SNAP on or off; F8 and Ctrl + B are toggle keys you can use even in the middle of another command. You can tell if SNAP is on by looking at your screen:

> **R12DOS**, **R13DOS:** When SNAP is on, the word SNAP is in the upper left corner of your screen.
>
> **R12Win**, **LT:** When SNAP is on, the S button in the toolbar appears to be depressed. You can also toggle SNAP on and off by clicking on this button.
>
> **R13Win:** When SNAP is on, the word "snap" is emphasized in the display bar at the bottom of the screen. You can also toggle SNAP on and off by double-clicking on this button.

The next two drawing aids do not require values; they are either on or off. Although present in the dialog box, they are usually more easily invoked from the keyboard via function keys or Ctrl + key combinations.

ORTHO

If you start to draw a line segment and have ORTHO on when you select the other end of the line, AutoCAD draws a line that is perfectly horizontal or perfectly vertical, regardless of where you pick the next point. Watch the elastic line while you move the mouse around. At what point does it snap from horizontal to vertical?

Draw several connected lines, using F8 or Ctrl + O (the letter O, not the number zero) to toggle ORTHO on and off as you go.

> **R12DOS:** When ORTHO is on, the word ORTHO is in the upper left corner of your screen.

> **R12Win**, **LT:** When SNAP is on, the O button in the toolbar appears to be depressed. You can also toggle the ORTHO mode by clicking on the O button.

> **R13Win:** When ORTHO is on, the word "ortho" is emphasised in the display bar at the bottom of the screen. You can also toggle ORTHO on and off by double-clicking on this button.

When on, ORTHO applies to all commands for which AutoCAD asks a second point, including LINE, ARC, CIRCLE, MOVE, COPY, MIRROR, ARRAY, and ROTATE. Thus lines that are drawn will be exactly horizontal or vertical, moves and copies will take place in exactly horizontal or vertical directions, the imaginary line around which you are mirroring will be horizontal or vertical, and so on.

In order to simplify the initial explanation I said that ORTHO forces things to be horizontal and vertical; actually, it aligns with any rotation of SNAP that you may have set. Thus, in our earlier example of a building with one wing drawn at an angle of 37 degrees, if SNAP is rotated to this alignment then all lines will be drawn and all edits will take place at an angle of 37 or 127 degrees ($37° + 90° = 127°$). There is also another special case, which I will soon describe under "Isometric Snap/Grid."

Try this: draw a line with ORTHO on, but type in the exact coordinates. What happens? Because it is more work to type in a point's coordinates than to pick the point, AutoCAD assumes you *really* want that specific point. In this case it ignores both ORTHO and SNAP and draws the line using the exact specified coordinates.

Whenever I want to mirror/move/copy *exactly* horizontally or vertically, I always deliberately pick the second point "off square." Remember how AutoCAD allowed you to drag entities to new locations during the editing commands? If ORTHO is on, the image will only drag horizontally or vertically; if ORTHO is off, the dragged image will remind me that things aren't right. If I inadvertently had ORTHO off and by chance picked a point that was nearly square, I would almost certainly end up with something that looked right but was actually off by a small angle. This can cause all sorts of problems later.

BLIPS

Blips are the little white spots that appear whenever you pick a point on your screen. Using the BLIPS command or the {DRAW-ING AIDS} dialog box, you can turn them off so they don't appear; most users leave them on.

Solid FILL

This mode applies to wide polylines, which are covered in Chapter 9.

HIGHLIGHT

When you select entities for editing, they become highlighted (dotted) so that you can see what you have selected. Highlighting can take a lot of time if you have selected many entities in a big drawing and are running on a slow machine. Using the HIGH-LIGHT command or the {DRAWING AIDS} dialog box to turn it off does exactly what it suggests: entities are still picked, but they are not highlighted.

Isometric Snap/Grid

This is not a separate command but rather one mode of SNAP. It is closely related to ORTHO because it forces everything to a precise alignment. It differs from ORTHO in that it forces everything not to right angles but to the isometric projection angles. This mode is very useful for drawing isometric drawings (surprise!) such as piping layouts.

Invoke this mode by picking the ISOMETRIC square in the DRAWING AIDS dialog box. Picking Left, Top, or Right from the box flips you over to the appropriate isometric plane. Try drawing a cube by drawing suitable lines in each of the three planes.

Once in isometric mode, you do not need to bring up the dialog box to change isometric planes. Hit Ctrl + E at any time to toggle through them.

Keystroke Summary

You do not have to use the dialog box to turn settings on or off. The top three picks of the SETTINGS pop-down menu in R12DOS and R12Win will toggle them, as will the following function keys and Ctrl + key combinations in all AutoCAD versions:

GRID	F7	Ctrl + G
ORTHO	F8	Ctrl + O
SNAP	F9	Ctrl + B

All operate transparently and so can be done at any time, even in the middle of another command.

Object Snaps

It is now time to get into one of AutoCAD's most important drawing aids: object snaps. This aid allows you to have your selected pick point snap exactly to a particular point on a selected entity.

Whenever AutoCAD asks for a point, you do not need to pick or type in a point right away. Instead you supply at least the uppercase letters of a snap override mode (listed next). AutoCAD then asks for the point again, but when you pick it AutoCAD adjusts the location of the point to suit the mode you specified.

Here is a list of the snap override modes and what they do:

CENter	Snaps to the exact center of an arc or circle. This is used for drawing concentric circles, for example.

ENDpoint	Snaps to the closest end of a line or arc. Note that you can pick a line near its middle, but the pick point will be way out at the end.
INSertion	Snaps to the insertion point of a line of text or of a special type of entity called a "block," covered in Chapter 12.
INTersect	Snaps to the exact point at which two lines, arcs, or circles intersect or cross.

R12DOS, R12Win, LT: When picked, both objects must cross within the square pick box that appears where the cursor lines cross.

R13DOS, R13Win: If AutoCAD does not find a pair of entities that cross within the pick box, it will ask you to pick a second entity. If possible, it will find the point where they actually do intersect or where they would intersect if they were extended as necessary.

MIDpoint	Snaps to the exact middle of a line or arc.
NEArest	Snaps to the point on a line, circle, or arc that is closest to the cursor when the pick button is pressed.
PERpendicular	Drops a perpendicular from the previous point to the selected object. It will draw not only a line that is perpendicular to another line but also one that is perpendicular to an arc or circle. Note also that perpendicular does not mean just vertical; it also means at right angles.
	To see what I mean, refer to Figure 5-1, where you can see that the two lines in A are perpendicular; the two lines in B are perpendicular, even though they do not meet (C shows this); and the line in D is perpendicular to the circle and the arc.
QUAdrature	Snaps to the nearest 90-degree point (north, east, south, or west) of a circle or arc.
TANgent	Draws a line that is exactly tangent to or from the selected arc or circle.

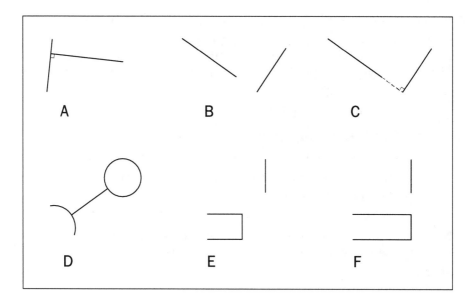

Figure 5-1: PERpendicular

Using snap overrides is not limited to entity creation. They can (and should) be used *any* time AutoCAD asks for a point (which includes the two points required to specify a distance), whether during a drawing operation or any editing command.

You can move a line so that its end lands exactly at the center of a circle, position a copy of a circle so that its north quadrature point coincides with the middle of an arc, and so on. Refer again to Figure 5-1. I modified the three connected lines in E using STRETCH. I then windowed the lower vertical line and the intersecting ends of the two horizontal lines. When AutoCAD asked for the "From point," I picked INTersection. When asked for the "To point," I replied PERpendicular to the upper vertical line. I ended up with detail F shown in the figure.

You do not need to type in the snap override. Whenever AutoCAD asks for a point or a distance during any command, you can instead click the middle button on a three-button mouse or the third (right) button on a digitizer puck. AutoCAD displays a popdown menu at the cursor location which lists all the snap overrides. Simply pick the desired mode.

If you have only a two-button mouse, you should get a three-button one. To use AutoCAD properly you should be using that middle button extensively to bring up the object snap menu. Meanwhile, you can pick the object snap modes as follows:

> **R12Win and LT:** Pick from the toolbox.
>
> **R12DOS, R12Win, R13DOS:** Pick {ASSIST} {OBJECT SNAP}, then the desired mode.
>
> **R13Win:** Pick {TOOLS} {TOOLBARS} {OBJECT SNAP} to pop up a toolbar of object snaps.

Note also that a snap override does exactly that—overrides and takes precedence over *any* SNAP or ORTHO modes that may be on.

OSNAP

This command was named after that famous Irish draftsman, Seamus O'Snap.

AutoCAD allows you to set running object snaps, which make AutoCAD automatically invoke the specified snap override for a picked point. OSNAP settings remain in effect until you change or reset them with another OSNAP command.

You can change running object snaps on the fly via a dialog box you bring up transparently. Follow these steps:

1. Start LINE and draw a few segments.
2. While you are still in LINE, do the following:

   R12DOS and R12Win: Pick {SETTINGS} {OBJECT SNAP . . . }.

   LT: Pick {ASSIST} {OBJECT SNAP . . . }.

   R13DOS and R13Win: Pick {OPTIONS} {RUNNING OBJECT SNAP . . . }

   A dialog box appears.
3. Pick one or two of the modes; as usual, the square boxes are toggles.

4. Pick OK. You are returned to where you left off, but now the selected object snap modes are active.

You thus could draw several line segments that automatically snap to the intersection points of a grid, then toggle over and draw several more through the centers of several circles, and so on. Just remember that any selected, running snap modes *will* remain active after you leave LINE and until you specifically turn them off.

Be aware that running OSNAPs can have another problem. They pick the *youngest* entity that meets the specification, which can make it difficult to pick an older entity. If the end of a selected line touches the end of a younger line, then the younger line will be selected instead. You will be unable to select the older line until you turn off the running OSNAP mode of END.

And Now for the Sermon . . .

SNAP, Snap overrides (OSNAP), and ORTHO are not just commands: they form a philosophy. A common mistake of beginners is not to use them, thinking that if things are lined up and look right to the eye, then everything will match. And why not? That assumption worked for old-fashioned pencil and paper (remember them?).

A quick look at a few numbers will reveal the root of the problem. A typical graphics screen has an image formed from about 600 horizontal lines in an effective working area about 6 inches high, after the status and command lines are removed. So you could expect to be able to pick a given point to within about 6/100, or 0.01, inch. The problem is, a typical machine shop works to 0.001 inch, and AutoCAD works to 14 decimal places. Thus two entities that appear to touch on the screen probably in fact do not if they were placed there freehand.

So you should use AutoCAD's SNAP/ORTHO/(snap) override facilities to ensure that everything matches.

You may still be tempted to ask, "What's the problem? If it looks close enough when plotted, it should be OK." However, not using the snap facilities at all times can cause several problems:

▶ DISTANCE and automatic DIMENSION commands (discussed in Chapters 13 and 8, respectively) will not yield the expected results. You may try to dimension something to be 0.625 units long, for example, but the automatic dimensioning function yields something like 0.623997246. As a result, you have to do a lot of rekeying to type over the default value, thus eliminating the advantage of having the computer do it automatically.

▶ When doing automatic cross-hatching, AutoCAD hatches everything inside the selected boundary. If there is even a minuscule mismatch (gaps or overlaps) at one corner, AutoCAD will probably mess up any attempt to cross-hatch it.

▶ When certain snap modes *are* used, they will fail. For example, if you try to snap to the intersection of two lines that don't intersect, there is bound to be trouble.

If you don't believe me, try it as follows:

1. Turn off SNAP and ORTHO.

2. Draw a line at an angle on your screen.

3. Terminate LINE.

4. Draw another line at a different angle, touching the end of the second line to one end of the first. Line it up as best you can by eye.

5. Do a ZOOM Window, picking a very small window that just encloses the point at which the lines touch.

   Surprise! I'll bet they don't touch anymore (if they still appear to, do another very small ZOOM Window).

6. Do a ZOOM All to show all of your drawing.

7. Draw another line from some arbitrary point. AutoCAD asks for "To point."

8. Enter the word END (or pick it from the screen or pop-down menu).

9. Pick one of your earlier lines at a point near one end.

Now you can ZOOM Window all day using ever smaller windows; the last two lines will always touch at their ends.

What happens if you try to draw a line tangent *from* a circle or arc, then tangent *to* a second circle? How about a line that is perpendicular *from* one circle and perpendicular *to* another? AutoCAD can do it, but the elastic line will disappear, because AutoCAD does not know where to attach it until you select the other end of the line.

Snap overrides are by far AutoCAD's most used and most significant feature. If you learn nothing else from this book than how to use them, I feel I will have done a good job teaching you how to use AutoCAD properly. You should be using an object snap override almost every time you point to a screen location with the mouse.

The mark of good CAD operators is the precision of their drawings. When inspecting an AutoCAD drawing, I first check to see that object snaps have been used. A drawing can be useless in many applications if they have not been. This is becoming especially true in mechanical design, where more and more often the machinist does not work from a paper drawing, but instead the AutoCAD file is fed directly to a computer–numerically controlled (CNC) milling machine. The CNC machine will object to things that do not meet, things that overlap, things that are not tangent, and so on.

This chapter covered drawing aids. They are what differentiate true CAD software from mere "picture-making" programs.

6 Layers, Colors, and Line Types

LAYER

It is common practice when producing paper-and-pencil architectural drawings to start with a base drawing that shows the basic building layout. A series of transparent sheets are then laid over the drawing, and separate subdrawings are made for the walls, the wiring, the plumbing, the ventilation, and so on. Layers can be stacked up to check for interference, or printed separately to give specific information to one subtrade. AutoCAD can do this, too, as shown in the simple sample in Figure 6-1.

Have you noticed that everything you have drawn so far, including circles and arcs, has been drawn with a continuous line in one color? So why did the sample drawing you opened in Chapter 3 contain many colors and several different noncontinuous line types? Depending on your graphics card, AutoCAD can display up to 255 colors. Graphics cards can actually show 256 colors, but AutoCAD automatically switches the display color for "white" depending on how you have AutoCAD's background configured; white entities will display as white if the background is black but will shift to black if the background is white.

AutoCAD also has available a library of 24 different noncontinuous line types, such as Hidden, Dashed, Dots, and Phantom. There are eight basic line types, plus half-scale and double-scale

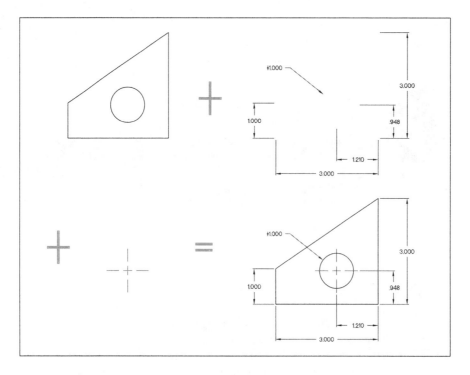

Figure 6-1: Layers

variants of each. R13Win and R13DOS add 14 more ISO standard line types to the library.

Open the same sample drawing you used in Chapters 3 and 4 and notice all the different colors and line types (you will be using this drawing throughout the chapter).

> **R12DOS, R13DOS:** From the menu bar, pick {SETTINGS} {LAYER CONTROL}.

> **R12Win, LT, R13Win:** Pick the Layer button at the left end of the toolbar.

A dialog box appears. A quick inspection of it reveals the obvious: it shows the name, state, color, and line type of every layer currently defined in the drawing. If the list is longer than one window can show, scroll through it using either the slider bar or the Page Down and Page Up keys on your keyboard.

The Current Layer

All drawing that you do, including lines, circles, arcs, text, and so on, lands on and takes the properties of the current layer. Obviously, only one layer at a time can be current.

To make a layer the current layer, follow these steps:

1. Pick a layer name from the list. It becomes highlighted, and most of the other pick boxes change from gray to black lettering to indicate that they are now active.

2. Pick the box that says Current.

3. Pick OK. You are returned to the Command prompt, and the name of the new current layer is displayed in the upper left corner of the screen. There may also be (depending on your hardware and your AutoCAD version) a small rectangle beside the name which shows the current layer's color.

Draw a line, and observe that it is not white and continuous. Instead it is the color and line type that the dialog box indicated were associated with the layer you selected as current.

R12Win, LT, and R13Win have a quick way of changing the current layer. Simply pick the window containing the current layer name (located near the left end of the toolbar), and a scrollable menu will pop down showing all layer names in the drawing. Pick a name and that layer becomes current.

Properties of Layers

In the opening paragraph of this chapter I described how architectural drawings were commonly created in the form of transparent overlays. Various aspects of a building can be emphasised or ignored by adding or subtracting the appropriate transparencies to the total drawing stack.

AutoCAD is able to perform the same action and several others, by setting various layer control parameters. Bring up the Layer Control dialog box again. Use your mouse to pick a layer name. When you do this, the six grayed-out action buttons in the upper

right corner of the dialog box become highlighted. We will now
work through each of the six choices to see how they work.

Frozen

When a layer is frozen, everything on it effectively doesn't exist,
temporarily. To see how this works, follow these steps:

1. Pick a layer name other than the current layer.

2. Pick FROZEN in the dialog box.

3. Pick OK. You will be returned to your drawing. Portions of it
   will seem to have disappeared.

Entities on a frozen layer cannot be seen or selected, so they
cannot be moved, copied, erased, and so on. Further, frozen layers will not plot. This feature enables an architect to create one
master drawing for a building; then, once everything has been
checked for interference, various layers can be frozen and
thawed so individual drawings can be plotted for walls, wiring,
plumbing, heating, and so on, all from the master drawing.

Frozen layers also don't regenerate or redraw, so you can speed
regens and redraws greatly by freezing layers you do not need to
see. For example, you might put a title block on its own layer so
it can be frozen while you do detail work on the drawing.

When you save the current drawing to disk, entities on frozen
layers are also saved, in their frozen state. You can thaw them at
any future editing session. Note that while only one layer can be
current, any number of layers in any combination may be frozen
at one time.

Thawed

This is obviously the opposite of frozen, making the invisible layers visible again.

Off

A layer that is off is semifrozen. It does not display or plot, and
entities on it cannot be edited. But it still contributes to regen
time. This mode is actually a holdover from earlier AutoCAD ver-

sions and has largely been supplanted by frozen layers. It is rarely used.

On

This takes layers that are off and turns them on again.

Locked

A layer that is locked is semifrozen, but in a different way. Entities on a locked layer display and plot, and you can use object snaps to lock on to a specific location such as the middle of a line. However, you cannot edit the entities on a locked layer.

Unlocked

Surprise, surprise! This will unlock locked layers.

And now for some general notes on layers and the Layer Control dialog box.

1. The current layer cannot be frozen.

2. Any number of layers in any combination can be frozen/thawed, locked/unlocked, and on/off at any one time. In an architectural drawing you might have the first-floor walls locked, the first and second-floor wiring on/thawed/unlocked, the third-floor plumbing current, and everything else frozen.

3. Within the dialog box you can pick more than one layer at a time. Picking a selected layer unselects it. When you pick any status, all selected layers will change to that status.

4. You can perform more than one change of status with one operation of the dialog box. You might freeze several layers, thaw others, lock/unlock some more, and change the current layer.

5. Nothing actually happens to your drawing until you pick OK. If you cancel, then anything you changed within the dialog box is ignored.

As well as the six status modes, there are two more properties of layers that can be set.

Color

Entities take on the color of the layer on which they exist. You can change the color of a layer or layers, and hence the color of their entities. Bring up the Layer Control dialog box and try this:

1. Highlight one or more layer names.

2. Pick the Set Color button near the lower right corner of the dialog box. A dialog box appears showing all 255 AutoCAD colors.

3. There are three different ways to change the color assigned to all selected layers:

   ▶ You can pick any one of the colored squares. When you do, a number will appear in the Color box at the bottom of the screen, along with a sample square of the color to the right of the number.

   ▶ You can pick the Color box and type in the name of one of eight standard colors (red, yellow, green, cyan, blue, magenta, or white). A small sample square appears after the name.

   ▶ You can pick the Color box and type in a color number from 1 to 255. The small square to the right of the name or number shows a sample of the selected color.

   If your graphics board cannot show 256 colors, AutoCAD approximates the shade as best it can. AutoCAD "remembers" the number of the actual color selected, so a drawing moved to a 256-color machine will be the correct color.

4. You can change your mind and select another color as often as you want. Once you get the one you want, pick OK to close the Color dialog box and return to the Layer Control one.

5. Pick OK again to close the Layer Control dialog box. All existing entities update to display the new color of their layer. If you change the color of the current layer, all new entities drawn will be the new color.

Plotting Colors

You should assign different colors to different layers even if you have only a monochrome monitor. When AutoCAD plots a drawing, it tells the plotter to use a different pen for each color. You could therefore install a thin pen in the first position of the plotter, a medium pen in the second position, and a thick pen in the third. When plotting, you can tell AutoCAD to use pen 1 for the red dimensions and text, pen 2 for the white object outline, and pen 3 for the blue drawing border.

Line Types

AutoCAD also uses layers to control the drawing of noncontinuous lines. The procedure is very similar to that used for layer colors:

1. From the Layers dialog box, pick one or more layer names.

2. Pick the Set Ltype button. A dialog box appears that shows all available line types.

3. Pick a line type that differs from the one specified for your selected layer or layers.

4. Pick OK to return to the main dialog box.

5. Pick OK to return to the drawing. Similar to when you changed colors, all entities on the selected layers are now of the new line type. All subsequent entities drawn on these layers will also be of the new line type.

Creating New Layers

Creating a new layer is simplicity itself, except for one minor detail. To create a new layer, follow these steps:

1. From the dialog box, pick the empty name box at the bottom.

2. Type in the desired name.

3. Pick the New button just above the name. The new layer name joins the others in the main layer-name listing box. By default a new layer is white and uses continuous-line type; you can now continue to assign it a line type and color as desired.

Layer Names

Many CAD systems only allow layer *numbers*. Make good use of the fact that AutoCAD allows layer *names*, which can contain up to 31 characters (but no spaces, question marks, or asterisks). Use descriptive names for layers, so that anyone can tell what is on them. It is a good idea to establish consistent names, colors, and line types within an organization.

When naming layers, it is a good idea to remember that you can use the standard * and ? wild cards when selecting layers later. This facility can be used to your advantage. For example, a single drawing of a ten-story building might have layers for walls, wiring, plumbing, text, dimensions, and so on. If you have ten sets of such layers (one per floor), each set numbered sequentially (for example, 01- through 10-), you can freeze all layers except those that start with 05-, and hence show only the fifth floor. Or you could freeze all ??-TEXT layers on all ten floors in one hit.

This grouped selection is performed using the Filters area in the lower right corner of the Layer Control dialog box. Pick Select and another box pops up. There are many choices on it, but I will walk you through one typical example:

1. Pick the Layer names box, and type in H*.

2. Pick OK to return to the main dialog box. The only layer names displayed will be those that start with an H.

3. Pick Select All on the lower left to highlight all of them.

4. You can now freeze, thaw, lock, unlock, change color, or whatever you want to the whole group at once.

5. In the Filters area, click On to return to the full list of layer names.

Line Types

Now we come to the one slight difficulty I mentioned earlier. If you start a new drawing and then create new layers in it, you will discover to your horror that "continuous" is the only type of line available. To use other line types, you must first load them in from an external file. Unfortunately, the menu picks to accomplish this vary greatly between versions, and they are not even available in R12Win unless the screen menu is turned on. Therefore it is easier to proceed as follows:

1. Enter the following command sequence from the keyboard:

   LINETYPE L *

2. A dialog box pops up. Pick OK to return to the command prompt.

Now when you select Set LType from the Layer Control dialog box you will have 24 or 38 line types from which you can choose.

You need to perform this operation only once on a new drawing. AutoCAD "remembers" the line type definitions when you save the drawing to disk. You also can do it on any existing drawing that does not already have the full set loaded in.

On the other hand, it is not necessary to load in the full set. In step 1 above you typed in an asterisk at the end of the command sequence. This told AutoCAD to load in *all* available line types. If you only want a few loaded in, you can type their specific names separated by commas, as in

HIDDEN,CENTER,DASHDOT

Line type definitions are held in external files. The dialog box in step 2 above listed any available line type definition files and defaulted to accepting the default file name. If you want to, you can experiment with any alternate files that appear.

Renaming Layers

When you pick an existing layer name from the dialog box list, the name appears at the bottom of the box. Move down and pick this box. You can then edit the layer name to anything you want within the 31-character limit. Remember, there must always be a layer 0 (zero), and you cannot rename a layer with a name that already exists.

When you pick the Rename button above the layer name, the name changes to the new value.

Changing an Entity's Layer

As you work on your drawing you may decide that one or more entities are on the wrong layer. AutoCAD provides a facility to change the layer on which entities reside:

1. Make the appropriate menu choice:

    R12DOS, R12Win: Pick {MODIFY} {CHANGE} {PROPERTIES}.

    LT: Pick {MODIFY} {CHANGE PROPERTIES}.

    R13DOS: Pick {MODIFY} {PROPERTIES}

    R13Win: Pick {EDIT} {PROPERTIES}

    You are prompted to select one or more entities. You can use the standard selection set–building procedures from Chapter 4.

2. When you hit Enter to complete the selection set process, a dialog box appears.

3. Click on the Layer button and a dialog box pops up showing all the layer names in the drawing. Pick one, then click on OK to return to the previous dialog box.

4. Click on OK to return to your drawing. All selected entities will change to the new layer; if the layer is frozen, the entities disappear until the target layer is thawed.

COLOR and LINETYPE

So far the only way you have specified the color and line type of an entity is by specifying suitable properties for the layer on which it resides.

AutoCAD allows you to specify a specific color and/or line type for an entity which is different from its host layer. The AutoCAD manual does not recommend your doing this, and only allows it for compatibility with older CAD systems that did not use layers. I DO NOT RECOMMEND IT. It is far less confusing in the long run to keep to the rule of one color and one line type per layer. If you want a new color or line type, create a new layer.

There are two ways to give entities a color or line type different from their layer's:

1. If you choose COLOR and enter a number from 1 to 255, or issue the command LINETYPE SET followed by the name of a loaded line type, then all subsequent entities you create will take on the designated color or line type. You can counter this action only by running these commands again and responding with a color or line type BYLAYER.

2. The Change Properties dialog box, which you used to change the layer of entities, also allows color and line type changes. Usually the only correct response is BYLAYER, so they will revert to having the properties of their host layer.

Properly used, layers are a very powerful feature of AutoCAD.

7 TEXT and DTEXT

As you may guess, TEXT is used to add text to your drawing. The basic command is very easy to use and extremely versatile.

TEXT and DTEXT Basics

There are actually two variants of this command. Earlier versions had TEXT, which is retained in later versions for compatibility. DTEXT, which stands for Dynamic TEXT, came along later. They operate the same way except for two minor differences:

▶ DTEXT shows each character on-screen as soon as you press a key. TEXT displays it only in the command prompt area, and AutoCAD waits until you enter the complete line of text before displaying anything on your drawing.

▶ With DTEXT, after you enter a line of text AutoCAD automatically drops down one line and prepares to accept another line of text, perfectly aligned below the previous one. TEXT, on the other hand, exits to the Command prompt at the end of each line of text.

Let's start with DTEXT. In all versions except R13Win you start DTEXT from the standard menu bar and its pop-downs.

R12DOS, R12Win, and R13DOS: Pick {DRAW} {TEXT} {DYNAMIC}.

LT: Pick {DRAW} {TEXT}.

R13Win: Move the cursor to the square in the {DRAW} tool-box that shows the letter A. Press and hold the left mouse button to make the flyout menu appear; while holding the mouse button down, move to the DTEXT square and release the mouse button (the default TEXT square invokes MTEXT, which we will cover later in this chapter).

Now carry on as follows:

AutoCAD asks this:	**You do this:**
. . . /<Starting point>:	Pick a suitable point with your mouse.
Height <.200>	Hit Enter (to choose the default).
Rotation angle <0>	Hit Enter (to choose the default).
Text:	A small square box appears on-screen. This box indicates the location and approximate size of the next letter. Type in whatever you want and observe as each letter appears on-screen. You can backspace over any errors as you go.

When you hit Enter at the end of a line of text, AutoCAD drops down a line, resets the square box to the start of the new line, and repeats the Text prompt. If you hit Enter on an empty line of text, AutoCAD drops out of DTEXT and returns you to the Command prompt.

Try this several more times, experimenting with the following:

▶ The insertion point can be specified by picking it with the mouse or typing in a coordinate pair.

▶ You can specify the height by typing in a number or picking a second point to "show" AutoCAD the height.

▶ You can specify the rotation angle by typing in a number or picking a second point.

▶ ORTHO, SNAP, and any running snap mode or snap override will affect any mouse picks you made to indicate the
insertion point, the size, or the rotation angle. You can thus
start the first line of text at the center of an existing circle,
for example.

▶ Hitting Ctrl + C to cancel the command deletes *all* lines of
text entered with the current run of DTEXT.

▶ There is a shortcut in DTEXT and TEXT. Recall that when
you hit Enter at the Command prompt, AutoCAD repeats
the last command, which in this case is DTEXT or TEXT.
When asked for an insertion point, if you hit Enter instead
of providing the point, AutoCAD selects a point just below
the insertion point of the last line of text entered. You thus
can insert more text that is perfectly aligned and spaced
below the previous line. AutoCAD assumes you want it to
have the same height and rotation angle as the previous
line, so it doesn't ask for these values.

Actually, it is even more clever than that. After you enter
some text, you can then draw any number of lines, circles,
arcs, and so on. If, when you later issue a text command,
you just hit Enter instead of specifying a start point,
AutoCAD will automatically select the correctly spaced point
below the last line of text you created.

Notice that I have used the word "insert" on occasion when refer-
ring to text creation. This is because you can use object snaps to
snap to the insertion point of a line of text. You can use this feature to return later and add a perfectly located line of text below
any previous line, not just the latest one.

Try this:

1. Start DTEXT.

2. When asked for the insertion point, snap to the insertion
point of the desired existing line of text.

3. Specify a height and rotation angle; you can probably hit
Enter at each of these prompts.

4. AutoCAD asks for the text. Do not type anything; just hit
Enter to return to the Command prompt.

5. Hit Enter twice, once to start DTEXT again and once to take the default insertion point.

6. Add your text. The new text is inserted perfectly below the selected one.

7. Hit Enter on an empty line to end the command.

Text Justification

AutoCAD does not require all text to be inserted from the insertion point. When you start DTEXT or TEXT, the initial prompt offers several other choices besides the insertion point. One of these choices is Justify, whereby AutoCAD allows you to select one of a large number of text alignments. These are not shown as menu picks, so you must enter them at the keyboard (you need enter only the uppercase letters).

Follow these steps:

1. Start DTEXT or TEXT.

2. Enter a J at the keyboard. A different prompt appears that offers the following variants.

Aligned	Align prompts for two points, then fits the text between them. The bad news is that if you put a little text in a wide space it grows very tall, and a lot of text in a small space gets very small.
Centered	Centered asks for a point, then centers the line of text around that point.
Right	Right prompts for a point, then *ends* the line of text at that point.
Fit	Similar to Align, Fit keeps the height constant but stretches the width to fit.

The preceding four modes all refer to the "baseline" of the text, which is the bottom of all the uppercase letters and the bottom of those lowercase letters that do not have "descenders," or tails.

| Middle | Similar to Center, Middle centers the text vertically about the center of the uppercase letters, as well as horizontally about the whole line of text. |

The alignment produced by the following modes should be fairly obvious from their names. Bottom modes align at the lowest point of the tail of a lowercase *g, j, p, q,* or *y,* and Top modes align at the highest point of uppercase letters. The middle modes refer to a point halfway between the baseline and the top. Remember, you only need to enter the uppercase letters to select a mode in reply to the Justify prompt:

▶ Top Left (TL)

▶ Top Center (TC)

▶ Top Right (TR)

▶ Middle Left (ML)

▶ Middle Center (MC), which is the same as Middle (M)

▶ Middle Right (MR)

▶ Bottom Left (BL)

▶ Bottom Center (BC)

▶ Bottom Right (BR)

Of all the modes, the default of left justified accounts for about 90 percent of usage. Centered and Middle (also known as MC) are useful for filling in the boxes in a title block, and account for most of the rest. The Aligned and Fit modes are least useful, because of the text distortion that occurs.

You have seen how DTEXT displays each character on-screen as you type it. To speed up its display, AutoCAD always shows text left-aligned. All the text in one run of DTEXT jumps to its selected alignment *after* you hit Enter on an empty line to end the command.

Recall I said earlier that if you hit Enter twice, you can add more text below the previous line. AutoCAD not only repeats the same text size and rotation angle, but

it also repeats
any alignments,
so centered text,
for example,
will continue
to be centered
on following lines.

Special Characters

Another useful feature is the provision of special characters not normally available on your keyboard. You can force a special character by including the following strings of characters in your text:

%%d draws a superscript degree symbol (°). Thus a line of text entered as "98.6%%d" will appear in the drawing as "98.6°."

%%c draws the circle or diameter symbol (ø).

%%p draws the plus/minus tolerance symbol (±).

Underscoring and overscoring can be toggled on and then off by including a "%%u" or "%%o," respectively, on each side of the text. The affected text can overlap, so some of your text can be both underscored and overscored at the same time. However, it is usually easier to use LINE and draw in the underscores and overscores later.

Let's Do It with STYLE

You may have noticed one more command choice at the DTEXT/TEXT prompt: Style. Before discussing STYLE, however, a quick look at fonts is in order.

Fonts

In typography, *font* refers to the general shape and style of text characters: are they composed of thick or thin lines, are they

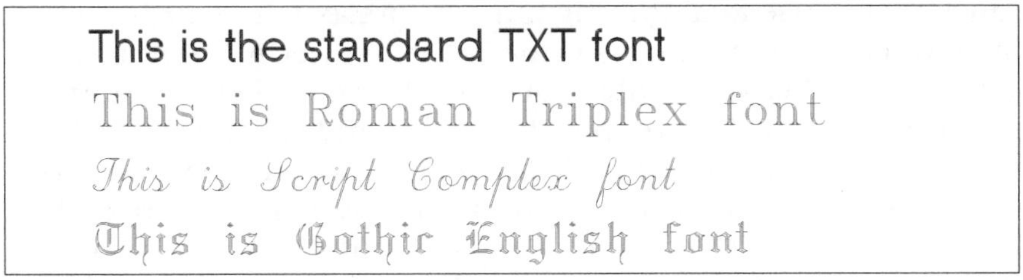

This is the standard TXT font

This is Roman Triplex font

This is Script Complex font

This is Gothic English font

Figure 7-1: Fonts

plain or fancy, and so on. Figure 7-1 shows four different fonts to help you see the difference. AutoCAD has many fonts:

> **R12DOS and R12Win:** Both come with nearly 60 fonts in AutoCAD's native format. The font collection contains basic fonts as well as "simple" and "complex" versions of them. The collection also includes several rather eclectic ones, such as Greek, Cyrillic, and symbols for mapping, astronomy, music, and mathematics. AutoCAD is also able to use Adobe PostScript fonts, and 16 of them are included with these versions.

> **LT:** LT comes with 40 fonts, a significant subset of the R12DOS/R12Win collection.

> **R13Win and R13DOS:** These come with about 100 fonts. As well as the native font format and Adobe Postscript fonts, these versions can also use TrueType fonts.

You can buy additional fonts from third-party suppliers who advertise in the AutoCAD specialty magazines, and you can import any standard Adobe PostScript font. R13Win and R13DOS will let you use the TrueType font files from your \WINDOWS\SYSTEM directory.

The font definitions are held in special files with the following extensions:

> .SHX AutoCAD's native format
>
> .PFB Adobe PostScript
>
> .TFF TrueType

Any font you use in a drawing must be present on your hard drive whenever the drawing is loaded into AutoCAD. If it isn't, you will be asked for a substitute font. However, before you use a substitute font, be aware that the widths and spacings of individual characters vary considerably among fonts. These variations can radically alter how text fits into your drawing. Generally, it's best to stick to the fonts that come with AutoCAD unless you have a specific need for something else. In particular, note that there may be legal implications regarding distribution of purchased font files if you send your drawing to someone else.

The font you use also affects how fast AutoCAD redraws, regenerates, and plots your drawing. Before you specify a font, find out how big its font file is. Go to the DOS prompt, change to the directory in which the font files reside (usually C:\ACAD12\FONTS, C:\ACADWIN\FONTS, C:\ACLTWIN, or C:\ACADR13\COMMON\ FONTS) and issue the DOS command DIR *.*

Look at the sizes of the font files. As a fairly firm rule, the bigger the font file, the longer AutoCAD will take to redraw, regenerate, and plot the drawing.

Creating Styles

Now that you understand what a font is, it is time to move on to text styles.

In AutoCAD, a style is a definition of a particular set of characteristics that determines the actual appearance of the text. It includes not only the font, but also the font size, height-to-width ratio, and whether you want the letters to be upright or slanted. You can even specify upside-down, backward, or vertical for specialized applications. Figure 7-2 shows four different styles, all based on the same font.

You can avoid having to go through the fuss of specifying these parameters each time you want to put some text on a drawing by predefining several styles and using them as required.

When you begin a new drawing, AutoCAD automatically creates a default text style called Standard. This style uses the font called TXT and has zero height (trust me), a width factor of 1, no slant, and is not backwards or upside-down. You will probably want to define several others of your own.

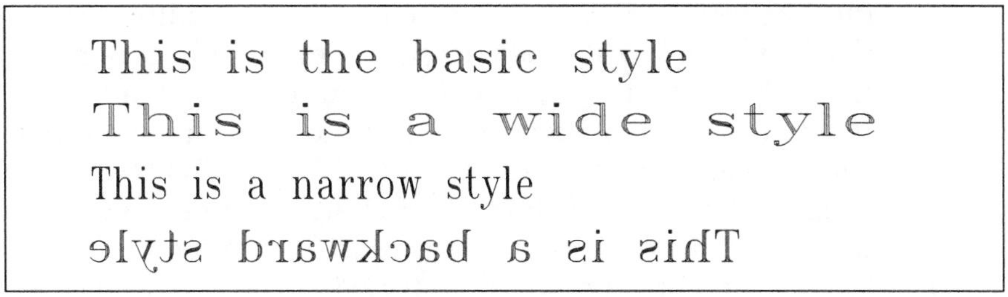

This is the basic style

This is a wide style

This is a narrow style

This is a backward style

Figure 7-2: Styles

The menu picks for starting STYLE vary considerably between the versions, and they are not always the easiest way to start this command. I usually find it easier to type in STYLE from the Command prompt.

To create a new style or to change the definition of an existing one, follow these steps:

1. At the Command prompt, enter STYLE.

2. AutoCAD will start by asking you for a name for your style. As usual when naming things in AutoCAD, you are allowed up to 32 characters for a style name. It is usually a good idea to select one that is long enough to be meaningful but short enough for quick typing.

   AutoCAD defaults to showing the current style name; if you hit Enter to take it as the default or if you type in the name of a style that already exists, AutoCAD will redefine the existing style parameters.

   If you redefine an existing style it will not have any effect on existing text, *except* for the fact that all existing text that was created using this style will update to using the new font.

3. Next you will be asked for a font to use. A dialog box showing all available font file names pops up; simply scroll through it and pick one with your mouse. You can also use the dialog box to browse through other directories.

4. Now you will be asked for a height for the text. Believe it or not, zero is a valid height. If you give a style a zero height the TEXT and DTEXT commands will ask for the height of

each text entry; if you instead specify a specific value, Auto-CAD automatically uses that height for every subsequent insertion of that text style. For most common applications you will use a standard text height in most of your drawings (⅛"?), so it makes sense to define your STANDARD style with this height. Note that the STANDARD style out of the box has a height of zero; if you use the STYLE command and set it to a finite height then you do not need to type in a height for every line of text.

5. Now you will be led through four or five quick prompts:

   ▶ Width? This sets the ratio of the characters' height to width.

   ▶ Obliquing angle? Do you want the text to lean forward or back?

   ▶ Backwards? If you reply Yes, your text will come out as a mirror image.

   ▶ Upside-down? Choose yes or no.

   ▶ Vertical? Not all fonts support text that appears in a vertical column rather than as a horizontal row. If the font you're using does, you will be asked if you want this mode.

When finished, you will end up at the Command prompt. The style you have just created or revised becomes the "current" style, so any text you now create will have the specifications you've just spelled out.

You will probably want to create several styles for small, medium, and large text and perhaps a few of the fancy fonts.

Changing Styles

If you have several styles defined, then you can select any one of them to be the current style as follows:

1. Start DTEXT or TEXT.

2. When the prompt appears, enter S for Style, then enter the name of the desired style. If you forget the name, enter a

question mark (?) to produce a list of all defined styles. DOS wild cards can also be used to produce a shorter list.

3. Carry on using DTEXT or TEXT in the normal manner. All text you create will be defined by the current style. If you perform other commands or exit AutoCAD and return, AutoCAD will still remember the current style name, until you change it to another one.

This mechanism makes it very easy to jump from text style to style without having to go through a long specification process each time.

Styles you create apply only to the current drawing. They are saved with it so you do not have to go through STYLE again; they are available when you edit the drawing later. In Chapter 14 I will show you how to customize AutoCAD so any styles that you have defined will be automatically available in *any* new drawing.

Renaming Styles
RENAME will allow you to rename any existing text styles.

Now that I have covered the fundamentals (and most of the fine print) of text, let's move on to a couple of menu-driven features that can simplify some of these processes.

Text Editing

We never make mistrakes. . . . There are several different aspects of text that can be defined and several ways of changing them. If all you want to do is move text to a different location, you can use MOVE or grip editing (covered in Chapter 4). Other editing depends on the version:

R12DOS and R12Win:

1. Pick {MODIFY} {ENTITY}.
2. You are prompted to select an entity; pick a text item.
3. A dialog box will appear. With this box you can change *any-thing* about a text entity—its layer, height, location, wording, style, and so on.

4. When you are finished, pick OK. All changes are applied to the selected entity, and you are returned to the Command: prompt.

LT: Text editing is quite limited. Follow these steps:

1. From the full menu, pick {MODIFY} {EDIT TEXT}.

2. You are prompted to select a text entity; pick one.

3. A dialog box will appear that lets you change the text wording.

4. Make any changes and pick OK. AutoCAD applies your changes to the text. It then loops back and asks you to select another text item for editing.

5. Hit Ctrl + C or pick a different entity to break out of the loop.

R13DOS and R13Win:

1. Pick the {PROPERTIES} button from the right end of the main toolbar.

2. You will be asked to select objects (plural); pick a single text entity and hit Enter.

3. A dialog box will appear. With this box you can change *anything* about a text entity—its layer, height, location, wording, style, and so on.

4. When you are finished, pick OK. All changes are applied to the selected entity, and you are returned to the Command prompt.

Note: If you pick more than one entity, you will get a much smaller dialog box that only lets you change the layer, color, and a few other properties. When you pick OK, the changes will be applied to all entities that you selected.

MTEXT

This R13DOS and R13Win command starts a dialog box that creates a Multiple *text* entity. This appears to be a series of separate text lines, but actually it is a single "paragraph" entity. It works much like a word processor; you specify a rectangular region for text in your drawing, and then as you enter or edit text it will "wrap" automatically within the rectangular region. This is a more advanced feature that you may want to explore on your own using the AutoCAD manual.

Large Quantities of Text

If you want to insert a lot of text, such as detailed specifications and notes on an architectural drawing, there are three different methods, depending on your AutoCAD version:

R12DOS and R12Win: It is best to create and edit the text in your favorite word processing program and save it as an ASCII or DOS text file. You can then import the file into AutoCAD by picking {DRAW} {TEXT} {Import text}. This will ask you several questions regarding the text file name, the style you want to use, the location within your drawing, and the justification. It will then inhale your text file into AutoCAD, where each line becomes a separate text entity.

R13DOS and R13Win: Remember when I instructed you earlier in this chapter to activate the flyout menu and then pick the {DTEXT} button? The default {TEXT} button in the {DRAW} toolbox starts MTEXT. The best way to insert large quantities of text is to create and edit it with your favorite word processor, save it as a "generic word processor" file, then use MTEXT to inhale it.

Text versus Layers

Text differs somewhat from other entity types. As you saw in Chapter 6, entities usually take on the color and line type of their host layer. Text, however, takes on only the layer's color. It does *not* take on the line type of its layer. The actual text characters are always drawn with a continuous line; you cannot draw any of the standard fonts with a noncontinuous line.

Spelling Checker

R13DOS and R13Win include a spelling checker, which you invoke by picking the button near the left end of the toolbar. It will ask you to select entities and will filter out any that are not text. It stops on any words that are not in its dictionary and will offer its best guess of what you really wanted. The dictionary is remarkably complete.

This chapter outlined the major points about text and text editing. As always, the best way to learn is to practice and experiment. You can't really break anything, and the DON'T PANIC note in Chapter 2 will always bail you out of any problem situation.

8 Dimensioning

If you were crazy enough, you could do all your dimensioning in AutoCAD the way you used to with pencil and paper, drawing each line, arrowhead, and number individually. But AutoCAD has a better way.

Start a new drawing. Turn ORTHO on (hit F8 or Ctrl + O) and draw a series of zigzag lines from the upper left to the lower right corner of your drawing, like a staircase. You should end up with six or eight steps of varying size; some should be wide and shallow, others narrow and tall, as shown in Figure 8-1.

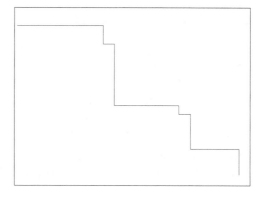

Figure 8-1: Draw some lines . . .

Before you start dimensioning, note that any dimension text will be drawn in the style that was last used under the TEXT command. If you were last using something odd like Gothic, you will probably want to return to the Standard style before you start.

As usual, the method of starting dimensioning commands varies between versions:

R12Win, R12DOS, R13Win: Pick {DRAW} from the menu bar, then {DIMENSIONS} from near the bottom of the pop-down menu. This will produce a submenu of dimensioning commands.

R13Win: Pick {TOOLS} from the menu bar, then {TOOLBARS} and {DIMENSIONING} from the pop-down menu. This will pop up the Dimensioning toolbar, which contains the dimensioning commands.

LT: Pick {DRAW} from the menu bar. The dimensioning commands will all be visible in a group at the bottom of the pop-down menu.

Note: From now on, as I take you through each dimensioning command I will assume that you have performed the appropriate menu picks to get to the dimensioning menu or toolbar each time.

Linear Dimensioning

AutoCAD has several modes available for linear dimensioning (as opposed to using angles, arcs, or circles). The earlier versions use separate commands for horizontal and vertical dimensions, but R13DOS and R13Win use a single command for both.

Horizontal Dimensioning

Once again, let's use our familiar columnar format to indicate AutoCAD's prompts and your replies. Figure 8-2 shows what you will be doing.

AutoCAD asks this:	You do this:
Command:	**R12DOS, R12Win, R13DOS, and LT:** Pick {LINEAR}, then {HORIZONTAL}.
	R13Win: Pick {LINEAR}.
First extension line origin or RETURN to select:	Hit Enter.

Select line, arc, or circle:	Use your mouse to pick a *long* horizontal line on your screen.
Dimension line location:	Pick a point above the selected line. This point is where the dimension line will land.
Dimension text \<length\>	The default value between the angle brackets < > is the length of the line as measured by AutoCAD. You may type in any value you want, and/or any text notes such as "REF" or "TYP," or hit Enter to accept the default value. This time, just hit Enter and watch the magic!
Command:	**R12DOS, R12Win, and LT:** Pick {LINEAR}, then {HORIZONTAL} (to repeat the command).
	R13DOS, R13Win: Hit Enter (to repeat the command).
First extension line origin or RETURN to select:	Hit Enter.
Select line, arc, or circle:	Pick a *short* horizontal line.
Dimension line location:	Pick a location.
Dimension text: \<length\>	Hit Enter to accept the default value.

Notice how the two dimensions differ, as shown in Figure 8-2. If there is not enough room to put the arrowheads and dimension text between the extension lines, then AutoCAD puts them outside the lines.

That works fine for dimensioning a single line, but how about extending the length over several steps? No problem. You can specify the exact points you want to dimension between. (This is

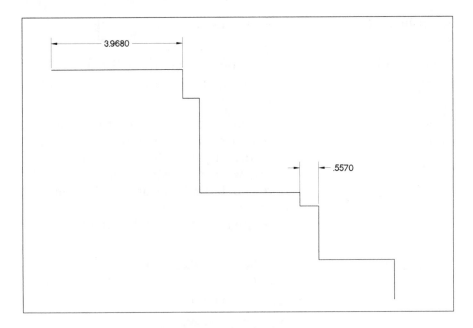

Figure 8-2: Horizontal dimensioning

one of those occasions where OSNAP settings and/or object snap overrides become mandatory.)

In the following exercise, you *must* use snap overrides. You can type them in if you want, but it is easier to use the menu picks: just hit the *middle* button on your mouse to pop up a menu. If your mouse or digitizer puck does not have at least three buttons, the easiest way to get at the object snap overrides is as follows:

> **R12DOS, R13DOS:** Pick the line of asterisks ***** at the top of the screen menu to bring up a submenu of object snaps.

> **R12Win; LT:** Pick the appropriate object-snap icon from the toolbox.

> **R13Win:** Pick {TOOLS} {TOOLBARS} {OBJECT SNAPS} to bring up the Object Snap toolbar.

Here we go. You will be dimensioning over several horizontal lines at one time.

AutoCAD asks this:	You do this:
Command:	**R12DOS, R12Win, R13DOS, and LT:** Pick {LINEAR}, then {HORIZONTAL}.
	R13Win: Pick {LINEAR}.
First extension line origin or RETURN to select:	Pick END. (You want to be exactly at the END of a line.)
end of?	Pick a line near one end (for example, point P1 in Figure 8-3).
Second extension line location:	Pick END.
end of?	Pick an end of a different line (for example, near point P2 in Figure 8-3.)
Dimension line location?	Pick a point above the two lines.
Dimension text? <length>	Hit Enter to accept the default value.

Figure 8-3 shows how AutoCAD gives you the total distance between the two points.

The first method—just hitting Enter and then picking a line—is great for a single line, but the second method is the only one that works over points that are not on the same line.

Go ahead and experiment with a few more horizontal dimensions. Can you figure out how AutoCAD decides where to put the text on a small dimension?

Vertical Dimensioning

Not unexpectedly, vertical dimensioning works almost exactly the same way as horizontal dimensioning; the only difference is that by default the dimension text remains horizontal instead of aligning with the dimension line. This is shown in Figure 8-4.

R13DOS, R13Win: As indicated earlier, these versions do not have separate commands for vertical and horizontal di-

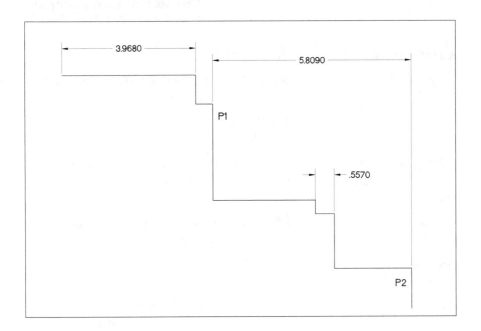

Figure 8-3: DIMensioning over several items

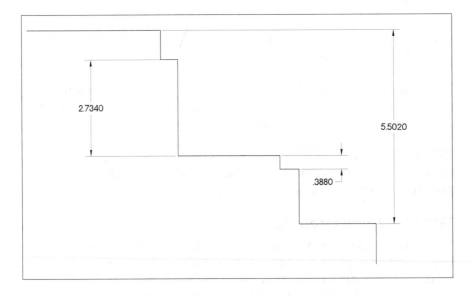

Figure 8-4: Vertical dimensioning

mensioning. Instead, AutoCAD is able to infer which one
you want from where you picked the dimension line location: if you picked a point above or below the line being dimensioned, AutoCAD creates a horizontal dimension; if you
picked a point to the left or right, it creates a vertical one.
An elastic image of the proposed dimension shows you what
AutoCAD intends to do as you move the mouse around prior
to picking the location.

BASE (Baseline)

Baseline dimensioning will automatically continue a series of
dimensions from a common baseline. For example, create a horizontal dimension on one of your horizontal lines near the left
edge of your drawing, but be sure to pick the left end of the line
first. Now pick BASE, and AutoCAD will ask for a single point.
Pick the end of a line that is beyond the right end of the first one,
and watch AutoCAD give a total dimension from the left end of
the first line (as shown in the upper portion of Figure 8-5).

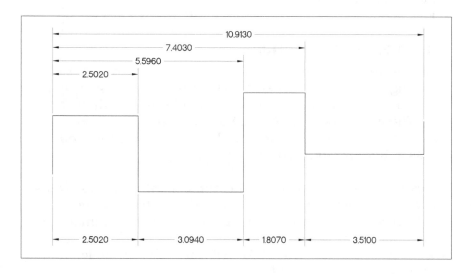

Figure 8-5: Baseline dimensioning and CONT

CONT (Continue)

CONT produces an effect very similar to BASE, except that each
succeeding dimension continues from the end of the previous
one, instead of adding to it. See the lower portion of Figure 8-5.

BASE and CONT will both work in vertical and horizontal modes. You must start from either horizontal or vertical first, then carry on with BASE or CONT. The direction in which either command proceeds is determined by the sequence in which the first two points were picked.

Aligned Mode

With AutoCAD you can place linear dimensions that are aligned with an angled line. By now you should be able to draw a line 2 units long at a 30-degree angle, then put three dimensions on it that show the rise (vertical), the run (horizontal), and the length (aligned) of the line. All are shown in Figure 8-6.

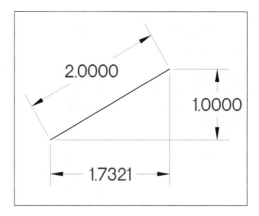

Figure 8-6: Aligned mode

"Steering" Text Location

I will now answer the question I posed a few paragraphs back regarding location of dimension text. Draw or find a short horizontal line, say 0.1 units long. Now put a horizontal dimension on it. There isn't room for AutoCAD to put the number and the arrowheads between the extension lines, so it puts them outside, just as a draftsperson would.

You can control the position of the number with the picking sequence. If you pick the left end first and then the right end, AutoCAD will continue left to right and will put the number to the right of the extension lines. The converse is also true; if you pick the right end first, AutoCAD will carry on right to left and will put the number to the left.

In vertical mode, the steering action is similar, with one added twist: "downward" dimensions place the number down and to the *left*, while "upward" ones go up and to the *right*.

Adding More Text

Whenever dimensioning is measuring a distance, it presents you with the measured value enclosed in angle brackets < >. At this point you have three choices:

1. You can hit Enter to take the default value.

2. You can type in something else and override the present value.

3. You can type in additional information to add to the default. You do this by typing in any desired prefix, a pair of angle brackets, and any desired suffix. AutoCAD will then create the dimension with your prefix, the default value, and your suffix. For example, if AutoCAD measures a length as <3.000>, then you can type in

    MILL <> TYP

    and AutoCAD will generate a dimension that says

    MILL 3.000 TYP

Angular Dimensioning

With AutoCAD, you can also dimension angles between lines. If your screen does not currently show two nonparallel lines, take a moment and draw some. From the dimensioning menu, pick {ANGULAR}. The new prompt indicates that there are four modes available. I will cover all four, but the first two are used the most.

Two Lines Mode

This is the default mode. Simply pick any Line entity, and Auto-CAD will ask you to select another. Do so, and AutoCAD will ask for the "Dimension arc location."

AutoCAD now attaches an elastic arc to the two lines to show you where the dimension will land. The significant point here is that you are not only selecting the radial location for the dimension arc, you are also defining which of the four possible angular dimensions will be the one drawn. Note that in this mode AutoCAD will not create a dimension larger than 180 degrees—it will draw extension lines as needed to ensure that the resultant dimension is less than 180 degrees. Figure 8-7 shows the four possible angular dimensions between two lines.

Now AutoCAD will offer the measured angle, enclosed in angle brackets < >, as the default value. As with linear dimensioning, you can just hit Enter to accept it, or you can type in a new value.

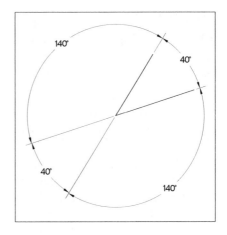

Figure 8-7: 2-Line angles

> **R12DOS, R12Win, and LT:** AutoCAD asks you for a "Text location." Normally you can just hit Enter to accept the default location (centered within the dimension arc), but if necessary you can locate it elsewhere.

> **R13DOS and R13Win:** AutoCAD does not ask for a text location; it always locates it automatically.

Now AutoCAD will draw extension lines if needed, draw a dimension arc through the selected "Dimension arc location" point, draw arrowheads at each end of the arc, and fill in the text.

Three Points Mode

This mode comes into play when you hit Enter instead of selecting the first line.

AutoCAD will ask you to select a vertex; point P1 in Figure 8-8 shows a typical example. Once you select the vertex point, AutoCAD attaches an elastic line to it and asks for a first endpoint. Select one such as point P2 in Figure 8-8. The elastic line remains attached to the vertex, and AutoCAD asks for the other endpoint (such as point P3 in Figure 8-8).

AutoCAD then carries on with the normal angular dimensioning prompts, and it dimensions things as though the imaginary lines defined by the vertex and the two endpoints actually existed. Snap overrides may be used.

This mode is most useful when dimensioning the angle to a component of a "block" (blocks are covered in Chapter 12). You cannot select a separate line within a block, but you *can* snap to its ends and hence define the vertex and endpoints for an angular dimension.

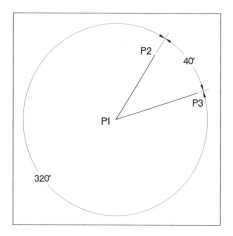

Figure 8-8: A three-point angle

There is one major difference between two lines mode and three points mode. The former has four possible angles and will not show a dimension greater than 180 degrees (Figure 8-7), while the latter has only two possible angles and *does* show angles larger than 180 degrees (Figure 8-8).

The two less commonly used angular dimensioning modes are the arc mode and circle mode.

Arc Mode

Having started the angular dimensioning command, simply pick an arc. AutoCAD automatically knows that you want to dimension it and so will dimension the angle defined by two imaginary lines drawn from the center of the arc to each end of it.

Circle Mode

This mode is probably the least useful. If you select a circle, AutoCAD snaps to a point on the circumference of the circle and uses it as one end of an imaginary line. The center of the circle becomes the vertex, and AutoCAD asks for the second angle endpoint to locate the other end of the second imaginary line. The second endpoint need not lie on the selected circle. The problem is, you have to select the circle and the first angle endpoint at the same time. QUAD is probably the only snap override that is effective in this mode; if you try to select the point that is at the intersection of a line and a circle, then AutoCAD selects the younger entity. If that happens to be the line, then you cannot select the circle.

Diameter and Radius

There are three ways of dimensioning circles and arcs.

Linear Mode

This mode is the same mode we used for dimensioning horizontal and vertical lines. In that exercise I told you to hit Enter and then select a line to be automatically dimensioned. If you select a circle instead, AutoCAD automatically dimensions it along a vertical or horizontal diameter, as shown along the top of Figure 8-9.

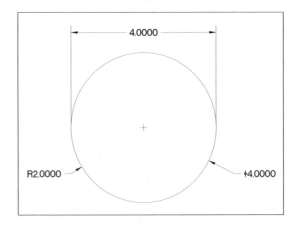

Figure 8-9: Dimensioning a circle

If you select an arc, it is dimensioned between the ends of the arc and/or the quadrature points, whichever is greater.

Diameter Mode

From the dimensioning menu, pick {RADIAL} and then {DIAMETER}. You will now be prompted to select a circle or arc. Do so, and you will be prompted to indicate a leader length. You can move the mouse to stretch the elastic leader out to a suitable location, but if you just hit Enter, AutoCAD will draw a radius leader that is two arrowheads long.

In either case, AutoCAD will give you a chance to add to or revise the default dimension in exactly the same manner as we have seen with the other modes. As AutoCAD fills in the default text, it automatically adds the ø symbol ahead of the text (as shown in the lower right portion of Figure 8-9).

Radius Mode

The radius mode is exactly like the diameter mode, except it measures the radius and puts an R in front of it, as shown in the lower left portion of Figure 8-9.

In both the diameter and radius modes, the leader extends the imaginary line connecting the center with the picked point on the circumference. A radius dimension can lie inside or outside an arc or circle, but a diameter dimension must lie outside. In any event, the leader line must be at least one arrowhead long.

Ordinate Dimensioning

This dimension-ing mode is com-monly used in machine-shop drafting. It pro-duces a single dimension num-ber at the end of a horizontal or vertical leader line. The number indicates the or-dinate (X or Y) distance from the origin (point 0,0) of your drawing. Figure 8-10 shows a typical example of ordi-nate dimensioning.

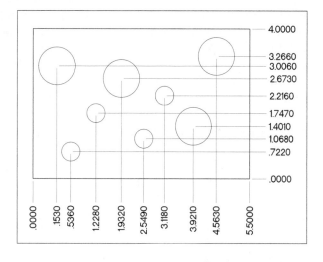

Figure 8-10: Ordinate dimensioning

When invoked, this mode asks you to "Select Feature." This re-quest may be slightly misleading at first, because it implies that you can simply point to an entity and pick it. The bad news is that the dimension is taken from the picked point, not from any entity you may think you have selected. The good news is that object snaps apply.

AutoCAD then prompts you to pick the leader endpoint and to choose whether you want the X datum or the Y datum dimension. If you select neither but instead just pick a point, AutoCAD assumes you want the horizontal dimension if the leader is vertical, and vice versa. This will probably be correct 99.9 percent of the time, but it can be overridden for the other 0.1 percent.

AutoCAD only supplies the absolute value of the dimension (that is, it does not show the negative sign if you go below or left of the origin), and it does not automatically indicate the origin. To avoid confusion, you will probably want to deliberately dimension or otherwise indicate where the point 0,0 is on your drawing.

By default, the ordinate dimensions are measured from the origin of the drawing, but you can change this if you want. AutoCAD has a command called "User Coordinate System" (UCS), which is used mostly for three-dimensional work. Among other things, it can set a temporary origin that is different from the main drawing origin. From the Command prompt, enter UCS and then Origin. Pick or otherwise define a point, and that point will become the new origin for ordinate dimensioning. When you have finished dimensioning, you can type the command sequence "UCS World" to return to the "world," or original origin.

I created the sample drawing in Figure 8-10 by setting the running object snap (OSNAP) to CENter so that ordinate dimensioning would automatically find the center of each circle as I picked it.

Center Lines

AutoCAD will automatically draw a set of center lines in a circle or arc.

> **R12DOS, R12Win, R13DOS and LT:** From the dimensioning menu, pick {RADIAL}, then {CENTER MARKS}.

> **R13Win:** From the {DIMENSION} toolbar menu, pick {CENTER MARKS}.

AutoCAD will ask you to pick a circle or an arc. It will automatically draw a center tick (a pair of short crossed lines) at the center of the selected item.

You can set the length of the center ticks by entering DIMCEN and replying with a value. Negative values are quite legitimate. If DIMCEN is negative, then AutoCAD does not just draw short center ticks but instead draws full center lines that extend outside the circle or arc by the specified amount. Try both cases and you will see what I mean.

Leaders

The dimensioning menus include a Leader command that lets you draw leader arrows and text all in one operation. You are prompted for a start point and then for intermediate points. If you hit Enter instead of picking a "Next point," AutoCAD draws one more short horizontal section to the leader line and then prompts you to supply the desired text. Sorry, you only get one line of text per leader, unless you are using R13DOS or R13Win.

Dimensioning Variables

Dimensioning can be fully personalized, as outlined in the AutoCAD manual. Depending on the AutoCAD version, there are forty to eighty different dimensioning variables that can be set. For example, you can select such factors as arrowhead type and size, extension line offsets, whether or not to generate concurrent metric dimensioning, whether the value breaks the dimension line or if it appears above it, ± tolerancing, high/low limit tolerancing, whether the text is always horizontal or aligns with the dimension line, and so on. You can even set separate colors for the text, the extension lines, and the dimension lines, so they can be plotted with different pens. A full explanation of all the variables is beyond the scope of this book, but the main thing is to be aware of the fact that they can be set if desired.

Dimensioning Styles

The concept is very simple, and it is exactly analogous to text styles.

R12DOS, R12Win, R13DOS, and LT: At the Command prompt, enter DDIM.

R13Win: From the Dimension toolbar, pick {STYLES}.

A dialog box pops up. Within it you can set certain dimensioning variables or pop up further subboxes with other dimensioning variables. You can assign a name to this particular collection of dimension settings, and you can repeat this process as many times as desired to set up several different named styles.

The next time you want to use the same combination of dimensioning variables, bring up the dialog box again and click on one of the existing style names. When you then click on OK, Auto-CAD will automatically set all of the dimensioning variables to match the saved set. This can be very useful if you regularly flip back and forth between standard, toleranced, and high/low dimensions, for example. The AutoCAD manual also suggests that you could establish various styles to match ANSI, JIS, and DIN standards.

There is one minor point to watch. If you have restored a saved style and then change even one variable setting, the current style name is no longer effective. This could present a problem if you make subsequent changes to any dimensions created after the change.

Editing Dimensions

STRETCH

AutoCAD dimensions are associative. This means that if you STRETCH a dimensioned entity, then the number in the dimension will automatically update to reflect the new size. Figure 8-11 illustrates this feature. Magic!

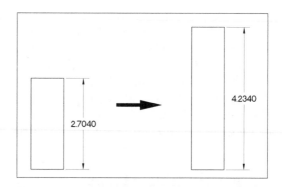

Figure 8-11: Associative dimensioning

You can also STRETCH the dimension itself if you want to move the extension line closer to or farther from the entity it dimensions.

TEDIT or DIMTEDIT

> **R12DOS, R12Win and LT:** Enter the commands DIM and then TEDIT at the Command prompt.
>
> **R13DOS and R13Win:** Enter the command DIMTEDIT from the Command prompt.

TEDIT or DIMTEDIT will let you easily change the location of the text within an existing dimension. Specifically, it will let you shift the text to the left or right end of the dimension line or select any arbitrary location for it.

If you move the text far enough away from its home location, AutoCAD automatically "heals" the dimension line to fill in the gap the text left. Conversely, moving the text back into the dimension line automatically splits the line to let it in. This occurs dynamically as you drag the text around. More magic!

You can also rotate the text to a specified angle within the dimension line. The Home option of TEDIT or DIMTEDIT snaps the text back to its default location and rotation.

Text Style and Size

There is one final gnarly bit to mention about dimensioning. I said at the start of this chapter that dimensioning uses the current text style. That is fine as far as it goes, but there can be a problem.

In Chapter 7 I mentioned that one of the things you can set with STYLE is the height of the text. Zero is valid (it's the default value); but if you leave it set at zero, AutoCAD will ask for a height for every line of text. If you set the height to be greater than zero, AutoCAD will use that height automatically and will not ask for a height for each line of text.

There is another good reason for specifying a fixed height for any style, and especially for the STANDARD style. Dimensioning uses the current text style to determine the dimension-text height. The problem is, dimensioning modes default to a fixed text height of .180 if the current style has a height of 0, but they use the same height as the current style if its height is greater than zero.

The really bad news is that if you have not redefined the current style to a specific height, then TEXT will ask you for the height each time and offer the default of .200. If you take this default, it is different from the dimensioning mode's default of .180, and both of these heights are probably too big anyway. A height of .125 is probably better in most cases.

The standard AutoCAD manual does an excellent job of explaining all of the subtleties of dimensioning. In this chapter I have covered the fundamentals that will apply to most of your work.

9 Polylines and Polyline Editing

"He was descended from a long line that his mother once fell for."

Polylines

Contrary to what you might think, a polyline is not something used by a parrot in a singles bar. The actual AutoCAD command is PLINE, pronounced "P-LINE," and the line it draws is called a *polyline,* or "pline" for short.

To see what a pline is, let's first look at what a regular line is not. When you are using LINE, you draw "From point:" and then "To point," "To point," "To point," and so on. AutoCAD draws what appears to be a continuous entity wandering across your screen, but in fact each segment of it is a separate line entity with its own start and end points. To AutoCAD, each segment was created separately and independently. It has no way of knowing that the separate segments were actually produced during a single run of LINE. Because each segment is independent, it can be edited individually.

On the other hand, a pline *is* what a single run of LINE *appears* to be: a single entity composed of a series of segments that are joined end to end. The points where the segments join are called the vertices.

When you MOVE, COPY, ERASE, and so on it behaves as a single unit, no matter which segment you select.

You may ask why AutoCAD has two different types of line entities. A pline can have several interesting properties that a line cannot, including a specified width that can vary from segment to segment and from end to end of a segment. It can contain arcs as well as straight segments, and AutoCAD can perform a variety of smoothing and curve-fitting operations on it.

As usual, the best way to learn about these properties is to dive in and try them. Follow these steps:

1. To start PLINE, do one of the following:

    R12DOS and R12Win: Pick {DRAW} {POLYLINE} {2D}.

    LT, R13DOS and R13Win: Pick {DRAW} {POLYLINE}.

    PLINE seems harmless enough at first. It asks for a "From point" just like LINE.

2. Pick a start point.

    AutoCAD returns with the message "Current line-width is 0.0" and a six-option prompt.

3. The good news is that you can ignore the options for now and simply pick several more points at random. The usual AutoCAD point-selection methods apply. You can pick points with the mouse, type in coordinate pairs, or indicate a rectangular or polar relative offset (example, @2.3<45) from the last vertex. All the object snaps, such as END, MID, and CENter, can be used. ORTHO and SNAP modes are still active if they are turned on.

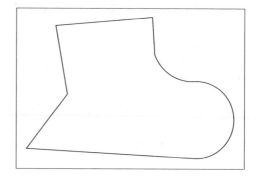

Try drawing a figure resembling that in Figure 9-1, starting in the lower left corner.

Figure 9-1: Polyline

Pline Arc Segments

The straight segments are easy enough, but how about the arcs? No problem. Just enter an A at the keyboard when you reach the appropriate vertex.

Your first attempt may produce disconcerting results, because this option appears to have a mind of its own. Unlike the usual ARC command, it defaults to asking for only one point. After you provide that point, an arc segment mysteriously appears with what appears to be a random radius and center location.

Closer examination of the pline arc reveals it is not as random as it first appears. The arc segment defaults to having a start direction that is tangent to the previous pline segment, whether it is an arc or straight segment.

The fun begins if you select an arc as the very first segment of the pline. In this case the start direction for the arc defaults to being tangent to the last pline, regular line, or regular arc that was drawn, no matter where that entity is located in the drawing. If no previous direction is defined, it defaults to the east direction.

Quite often this default direction is not what you want. You may want the first arc segment to start in some other direction, or you may want a hump in the line that is not tangent to the preceding and/or following segment. When you invoke the Arc subcommand, PLINE brings up a new prompt that offers several options. One of those is Direction, which, surprise surprise, lets you specify the starting direction for the next arc segment.

Plines have one interesting limitation: an arc segment of a pline cannot have an included angle of 360 degrees. Drawing an arc of 359.9999 degrees almost works, but it does leave a small gap in the circle. To draw a perfect pline circle, you must use the DOUGHNUT (or DONUT) command, which is covered in Chapter 10.

PLINE remains in Arc mode, drawing tangent arc segments, until you enter an L to return to Line mode. You can change from Arc to Line mode and back within a single pline whenever you want.

Terminating PLINE

When you get bored, terminate PLINE by hitting Enter or
Ctrl + C or by entering a C to have the pline close back to its
start.

Other PLINE Options

Now that you have drawn a basic pline, you are ready to move on
to the other options.

Start PLINE again and pick a starting point. This time let's take a
closer look at the six-option prompt that comes up. The options
are generally self-explanatory, so the best approach is simply to
experiment. A word of caution, however: read the prompts.
Often, choosing one subcommand from a prompt brings up yet
another prompt offering still more choices. We have already covered the Arc option, so let's go look at the other five. Being as
logical as usual, let's start with the last option.

Width

Herewith the first interesting property of plines: they can have
width. To see how this feature works, follow these steps:

1. Instead of picking the next point for the pline, enter a W at
    the keyboard to tell AutoCAD you want to set the width. You
    are asked for a starting width for the next segment. Note
    that the default width is zero; it produces a very thin line
    like that of LINE.

2. Type in a value, such as 0.2.

3. AutoCAD asks for an ending width and offers the starting
    width as a default. Hit Enter to take the default.

4. Draw more pline segments.

All segments will be the specified width, as shown in Figure 9-2.

After you finish drawing a pline that has wide segments,
AutoCAD bevels the ends of each segment so that they meet
cleanly at each vertex.

Figure 9-2: Wide PolyLINE

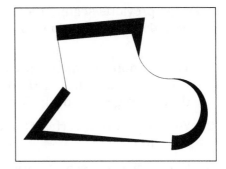

Figure 9-3: Variable Widths

Try these steps again, but as you draw the pline do not just select vertex points—stop occasionally to change the width. As you
can see from Figure 9-3, you can draw a pline with tapered segments, even when the segments are arcs.

AutoCAD "remembers" the current width. If you draw another
pline later, AutoCAD defaults to a starting width that is the same
as the width of the last pline segment you drew.

Halfwidth

Start a pline and invoke Width. Use your mouse to "show"
AutoCAD the desired width. Notice the rather odd action: the
"elastic band" stays anchored to the end of the last segment, and
you can pick only one point. The width then becomes the
distance between this point and the end of the segment.

Usually this is not the most convenient way to show AutoCAD
how wide you want the pline to be, so PLINE provides the
Halfwidth option. Invoke it by entering an H at the polyline
prompt. At first Halfwidth seems to behave like Width; the difference is that AutoCAD doubles the typed or picked distance to
generate the actual pline width. Experiment some, and you will
see what I mean.

Length

Length produces a segment of the specified length that continues
in the same direction as the previous segment. Why not just

make the previous segment longer, you ask? There are three reasons you don't want to do this:

1. The previous segment may have been an arc. Using Length, you can change from Arc to Line, then head off at a length that is tangent from the last arc segment.

2. You may want a vertex at a specific location so that you can snap to it.

3. Extra vertices become very significant when you do curve fitting, which I discuss later in this chapter.

Undo

This option behaves like the Undo option in LINE; it simply backs up one step and undoes that segment.

Close

Like LINE, Close creates one final segment from the current segment's end back to the start of the very first one.

If your pline has width and you want it to end up where it started, you are better off using Close rather than drawing the last segment back to the start, because then the ends will bevel properly. Curve fitting also behaves better with Close.

More Pline Tricks

Like other entities, a pline takes on the color and line type of the current layer and/ or can be assigned a specific line type or color. You can thus have a varying-width, meandering, dotted, dashed, or dotted-dashed pline, as Figure 9-4 illustrates.

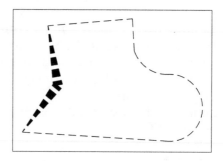

Figure 9-4: PLINE line types

While doing other drawing or editing, you can use object snaps and object snap overrides to snap to points on a pline. Each segment behaves as though it were a separate entity, so if you snap to the middle or end point of a pline you get the middle or end of the segment where you picked the line, not the middle or end of the complete pline.

The width is ignored, so the end of a segment is located at the center of the width. You cannot snap to the intersection of the corners of a wide pline segment, because in spite of its appearance, there is nothing intersecting there.

When you begin to dabble in 3D in AutoCAD, don't forget that you can give a pline thickness; the commands HIDE, SHADE, and RENDER (which are not covered in this book) will then treat it as though it were a solid object, especially if it also has width. Figure 9-5 shows a typical example.

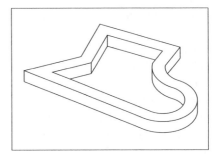

Figure 9-5: Solid PLINE

Editing Plines

I know that *you* never make ~~misteaks~~ mistakes, but sometimes the boss comes along and wants some changes made.

There are three ways to edit plines:

1. The standard AutoCAD editing commands MOVE, COPY, ERASE, MIRROR, and ARRAY work as expected on a pline as though it were a single entity.

2. Certain other standard editing commands, which I will discuss next, will change a pline,

3. There also is a unique PEDIT command to perform editing that applies only to a PLINE. I will discuss PEDIT after I discuss the standard commands.

Standard Editing Commands

STRETCH STRETCH relocates any vertex, segment, or group of segments while stretching the intervening segment(s).

OFFSET OFFSET produces a new pline that runs exactly parallel to the original pline, regardless of the twists and turns the original takes. Figure 9-6 shows how any width information in the original is carried over into the second line.

Figure 9-6: Offsetting a pline

EXTEND, TRIM, and BREAK These commands operate on a pline exactly as they do on a regular line or arc. A pline can be the boundary for any trim or extend operation. In any case, width is ignored and the operation takes place at the pline's center line.

FILLET and CHAMFER These commands operate on a pline, but with a twist. If you enter a P before selecting the pline, AutoCAD automatically inserts a suitable fillet or chamfer at every vertex down the length of the pline. Notice in Figure 9-7 how all four of the sharp corners along the left and top sides have become filleted.

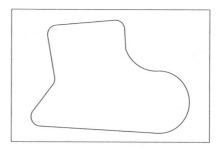

Figure 9-7: Filleting a pline

If you do not enter a P but just select a pline, AutoCAD asks you to select the second object. If the second object selected is the next segment along the line (in either direction), AutoCAD inserts a single fillet or chamfer between the two selected segments.

EXPLODE EXPLODE breaks up a pline into a bunch of discrete lines and arcs. Any width information will be lost, however. To access this command, pick {MODIFY} {EXPLODE}. Note that LT must show the *full* menu.

The foregoing list by no means exhausts the possible changes that can be made to a pline. For other editing to a PLINE, there is a specific command called PEDIT (short for PolylineEDIT).

PEDIT

PolyLINE EDIT, or PEDIT, is under the {MODIFY} menu. The actual name differs slightly in each version, but by now you should be able to figure out which one to use. (Just make sure that LT is showing the *full* menu.) To use PEDIT, begin with these steps:

1. Pick {MODIFY} {PEDIT}.

AutoCAD asks you to select a pline.

2. Select a *regular* line or arc.

AutoCAD tells you, "Entity selected is not a polyline." Now comes a surprise: by now you may have noticed that if you make a mistake during a command you will be dropped back to the Command prompt or asked to try again, but not in PEDIT. Instead it asks, "Do you want to turn it into one?" If you respond with a Y, PEDIT turns the line or arc into a one-segment two-dimensional pline. If you respond with an N the command will cancel itself.

Once you have a PLINE selected, either by direct selection or by conversion, then AutoCAD brings up a nine-choice submenu. As usual, you invoke any subcommand by entering any uppercase letters in the prompt.

eXit Hitting Ctrl + C, hitting Enter, or entering an X (for eXit) will return you to the Command prompt. Any editing that you have specified within PEDIT will be applied to the pline. This is a little different from most other editing commands, which ignore any specified changes if you cancel the command.

Close or Open Close or Open determine the pline's current status. Close adds one more segment from the end back to the start; Open deletes the last segment, creating a new end.

Join Join attaches existing entities onto the selected pline. You can use Join to turn two (or more) plines into a single longer one and to turn lines or arcs into pline segments and add them onto the selected one.

Having selected Join, you are asked to "Select objects." You can use any of AutoCAD's entity-selection mechanisms, and you can include the original pline or "illegal" entities such as text in your selection set. Entities need not be picked in any particular order.

When you hit Enter to terminate the selection process, AutoCAD begins sorting through the selected entities to find those that meet both of the following criteria:

- They are a line, pline, or arc.
- One end of the entity must *exactly* match one end of the pline. This is another reason why it is important to use object snaps and snap overrides when drawing.

AutoCAD repeatedly loops through the selection set applying these two tests to each selected entity; if one entity complies, it is added to the pline. The modified pline becomes the new second criterion for subsequent loops through the remaining entities.

Note the second criterion in particular. Entities that form a *tee* or don't touch are not added, so the pline will stop growing even though other entities in the set do meet the criterion.

Width Width allows you to specify a new width for the pline. Any individual segment widths or varying widths specified during the original pline construction are lost, replaced by the single, uniform width.

Curve Fitting

Now I'll throw a real curve at you. Fit and Spline turn a pline into a smooth, flowing curved line.

Fit Fit generates a curved line that passes exactly through every vertex of the pline, including the two ends. It does this by turning each line segment (whether straight or arc) into two arcs and inserting a new vertex where the two arcs touch. All arc segments are tangent to their neighbors right down the length of the line.

The result can be bizarre when using a pline with only a few segments, especially when the individual segment lengths vary considerably. The pline tends to get bumpy around the short segments.

When you fit a pline that had varying width information, each pair of new segments retains the total taper of the parent segment.

Spline Spline fits a Bezier spline, or "b-spline," curve to a pline. B-splines were first developed during the construction of wooden ships. Imagine a long, thin, supple wooden plank. Support it at each end, then hang weights on it at various points along its length. Some of the weights can be negative (a pulley can be used to create an upward force on the plank).

A spline-curved pline behaves the same way. The generated curve starts and ends exactly at the ends of the original pline, but it does not pass through the intermediate vertices; it only gets pulled toward them. The closer together and the more numerous the vertices, the stronger the pull. The curve that is generated is actually a new pline, consisting of a large

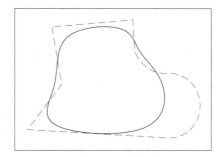

Figure 9-8: Spline curve

number of small arc segments; the underlying, defining pline becomes invisible. In Figure 9-8, the original pline is shown as dashed while the spline curve it generated is continuous.

If you spline a pline that had varying width information, the resultant curve tapers uniformly from the start to the end and any intermediate width information is ignored.

A spline curve generally produces a smoother shape than a fit one does. It also produces larger drawing files.

Within PEDIT, you can flip back and forth between Fit and Spline to see the difference between the two curve types.

If you are really curious, use the command SPLINETYPE, respond with a 5 or a 6, repeat the spline operation, and note the different form of the curve. (A setting of 5 produces a "quadratic" spline, while the default of 6 produces a "cubic" spline.)

Decurve As you might suspect, Decurve turns a fitted or splined curve back into the original pline shape—sort of. The decurving operation turns all the arc segments back into straight lines, so if the original pline happened to contain any arc segments, they also get turned into straight segments.

Decurving can be done at almost any time, even in another editing session, with one limitation: if you break or trim a fitted or splined curve, you will be unable to decurve it. It turns into a pline consisting entirely of arc segments, and the defining frame evaporates.

If you explode a fitted or splined pline, you get a whole bunch of regular arcs.

Undo Undo works as it does in LINE and PLINE: it reverses the most recent editing action. This can be repeated right back to the start of PEDIT.

Edit Vertex All the PEDIT options discussed so far apply to the entire length of the pline (you set a uniform width, or you fit a curve to the entire line, and so on). Edit Vertex, however, lets you attack the pline one vertex at a time.

When you select this option, an X appears at the start of the first segment visible on screen. The editing option is then applied to that segment. Next and Previous let you step backward or forward in the pline until you reach the desired segment. The default is the last of these two options used; you can hit N or P once, then Enter repeatedly to step along the pline.

Once again, selecting Exit or hitting Ctrl + C at any time aborts the edit in process and moves you back to the basic PEDIT command.

Here is helpful hint number one when editing vertexes on a long pline: do a ZOOM Window or ZOOM Dynamic to the general vicinity of the desired vertex *before* issuing PEDIT. Doing this will minimize the stepping you have to do.

This leads into helpful hint number two: you must use Auto-CAD's ZOOM Window or ZOOM Dynamic option. Otherwise, if you are using a display-list graphics card or ADI driver and use its "instant zoom," AutoCAD will still think you are zoomed back.

Vertex Editing offers several options. Their operation is generally intuitive, so I will hit just a few high spots as follows:

Break Break remembers the current vertex location and then prompts you to move to the next or previous vertex. You can repeat this action until you reach the desired vertex, at which time Go chops the original pline into two separate plines. The intervening segments will disappear.

Note the difference between the Break option of PEDIT's Edit Vertex option and the command BREAK: the Break option breaks a pline only at existing vertices, whereas BREAK creates new end and start vertices at the exact point you selected along a segment.

Here's helpful hint number three: You can snap to the end of a pline segment, so {BREAK} {END} {END} is usually faster than {PEDIT} {Edit vertex} {Next} {Enter} {Enter} {..... Break Next} Enter Enter {.... Go} {eXit} {eXit}.

Insert Insert inserts a new vertex downstream of the marked one. You are prompted for its location. The pline will then bend to pass through the new vertex.

Move Move asks for a new location and moves the marked vertex to it (but it is usually faster to use the grip editing operation from Chapter 4). From the Command prompt, pick a pline. Warm (blue) grips will appear at each vertex; pick one to make it hot (red) and stretch it to the new location.

Regen Regen regenerates the pline. This happens automatically when you finish editing. You also can use it if you want to see the effects of work in process without exiting.

Straighten Straighten operates like Break, except that instead of cutting out the segments that lie between two selected vertices, it turns them into one straight segment. If you select only one vertex and it is at the start of an arc segment, the arc becomes a straight segment.

Tangent Tangent enables you to specify a tangent direction. The curve-fitting options use this information to steer a fitted curve in a direction different from that which would normally be generated.

Width Width is a lot of fun. With it you can change the start and end width of the single segment that follows the X marker. Note that the effect will not be displayed on the screen immediately, but you can use Regen to force an update when desired.

As mentioned earlier, Exit returns you to the main PEDIT prompt, where you can continue with further editing of the current pline or use Exit again to return to the Command prompt.

Changing Layers

A PLINE moved to a different layer takes on the color and line type of the new layer, unless you have previously set its color or line type to a specific value.

Solid FILL

If your drawing contains a lot of wide plines, regens and redraws will slow down drastically because AutoCAD has to calculate all the pixels necessary to fill in the lines. There is a simple solution.

In Chapter 5 we discussed the "Drawing Aids" dialog box. One of the items in that dialog box that we ignored at the time was a button labelled "Solid Fill." Turn it off and plines (and dimensioning arrowheads) display as simple outline frames, which means they regen and redraw much faster than when Solid FILL is on. Note that the screen won't actually change until the next regen.

Solid FILL applies to plotting, too. You can do a quick check plot with it turned off and then turn it on for the final plot.

Summary

Neither regular lines and arcs nor plines are inherently superior. Each has its preferred uses, and each is "best" for specific applications. For example, if you want lines that are just a little bit wider (for example, heavier lines for a drawing border), you *could* use a wide pline. It is probably better, however, to use a normal line and put it on its own layer with a unique color. When you PLOT, use a thicker pen for that color. On the other hand, plines are better for curves, such as highways and contour lines, and for wide lines, such as printed circuit board traces.

10 More Entities

So far I have covered lines, circles, arcs, text, dimensioning, and polylines, which together will account for about 99 percent of your two-dimensional drawings. In this chapter I discuss three more entity types: the polygon, the ellipse, and the doughnut. However, as you will see, these are not really unique entities; rather, they are simply AutoCAD commands that quickly and easily construct these shapes from standard polylines.

POLYGON

For our purposes, a polygon is defined as a lumpy circle. In the bad old days BA (Before AutoCAD), it could be quite an undertaking to draw a polygon. Triangles and rectangles were rather trivial and simple, and hexagons and octagons were fairly easy, but drawing a 13-sided equilateral figure could turn into a career.

POLYGON solved this problem. The menu picks for this command differ in each version, so the best way to start is to type it in at the Command prompt, where it behaves almost exactly the same in all versions. After I explain the options and you play with them a bit, the menu picks are self-explanatory. To work with this command, follow these steps:

1. At the Command prompt, enter POLYGON. AutoCAD will reply by asking for the number of sides.

2. Enter the number of sides for your polygon. Note that AutoCAD obviously gets snarly if you try to draw anything less than a triangle; at the other extreme, it won't go above 1024 sides.

AutoCAD prompts for your choice from two options: Center and Edge. Let's try the Center option first, and then come back to study the Edge option.

Center

Center is the default mode. It is invoked simply by specifying a point. AutoCAD takes this as the center of an imaginary circle around or within which the polygon is to be constructed, as shown by point P1 in Figure 10-1 and Figure 10-2.

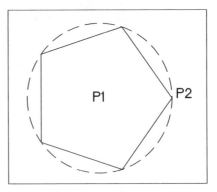

Figure 10-1: Inscribed polygon

The next prompt asks you to decide if the polygon is to be drawn inside or outside the imaginary circle. If you want it inside the circle, choose Inscribed; for outside, choose Circumscribed. (Note that LT does not have these choices; it will only draw Circumscribed polygons.)

Inscribed As shown in Figure 10-1, an inscribed polygon fits exactly inside the imaginary circle (shown by the dashed line), with the points of the polygon touching the circle. Point P1 defines the center of the imaginary circle.

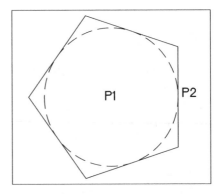

Figure 10-2: Circumscribed polygon

Circumscribed A circumscribed polygon exactly surrounds the circle so that the middle of each segment is just tangent to the circle. Figure 10-2 illustrates this; once again, point P1 is in the center of the imaginary circle. You can use this option to draw an even-numbered polygon with a required distance "across flats," such as for a bolt head.

Having specified the type of polygon, you will next be asked for the radius of the defining circle. If you move the cursor an elastic polygon follows it so you can see where things are going. As usual, you can "show" AutoCAD the radius with your mouse, or you can type in a value. As you can see from the two illustrations, the point P2 defines both the radius of the defining circle and the orientation of the polygon.

Edge

In this mode you define the polygon by specifying the two ends of one edge instead of specifying the center and radius, as shown in Figure 10-3.

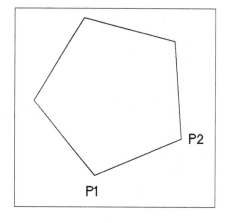

Figure 10-3: Edge polygon

1. Start POLYGON and specify the number of sides the polygon is to have.

2. Enter an E instead of specifying a center point.

    AutoCAD prompts you to specify the ends of one edge.

3. Define the first point, P1, and use the elastic polygon to drag the second end point into position (see Figure 10-3).

AutoCAD constructs the polygon in a counterclockwise direction. The length of each side is exactly equal to the distance between the two defining points, and the first side exactly aligns with the points.

The standard AutoCAD manual simply tells you to enter the two points required to define a polygon and then drag the second point into position using your mouse. It does not remind you of all the different entry modes that are available. I do that next.

As usual, you can mix and match any combination of typing-in coordinate pairs or picking points. SNAP, ORTHO, running object snaps, and snap overrides all apply. Relative coordinate distances (those preceded by the @ sign) are also legal for any point; the point will be located the specified x and y distances away from the previous point. The previous point need not be from the current POLYGON command; AutoCAD "remembers" the last point specified by almost any command, including that of the end of the last line, and so on.

Now that you have played with the basic command, here are the menu picks for starting it:

> **R12DOS, R12Win, and R13DOS:** Pick {DRAW} {POLYGON}. From the cascading menu, pick {EDGE}, {INSCRIBED}, or {CIRCUMSCRIBED} as desired, and then enter the number of edges.

> **LT:** Pick {DRAW} {POLYGON} from the *full* menu. The default is a centered, circumscribed polygon. Enter an E from the keyboard if you want an edge-defined one.

> **R13Win:** Pick {DRAW} {POLYGON} (initially, {POLYGON} will be found in the flyout under the {RECTANGLE} button) and follow the normal prompts.

Having drawn several polygons, you may want to edit them.

Editing Polygons

POLYGON does not actually draw a polygon; it draws a PLINE consisting of the desired number of equal-length straight segments. Once it is completed, there is no indication that the figure was ever anything except a pline. Figure 10-4 shows some of the editing that can be performed on a polygon.

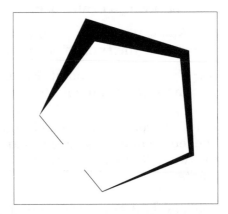

Figure 10-4: POLYGON Editing

PEDIT can be applied, in all its glory, to any polygon. You can specify a constant width for the entire line or vary the width from end to end for each segment. If any width is set to a nonzero number, the polygon is subject to the same fill-display state (on or off) as any pline.

You also can move vertices so that the shape is no longer a regular polygon, fit or spline-curve it, decurve it, and so on (if you fit or spline it while all edges are the same length it will look like a circle).

You can use BREAK to cut a random piece out of a polygon. A polygon can be trimmed, and it can also be the boundary for trimming and extending. You can snap to the end or middle of each segment. You can also fillet, chamfer, and offset a polygon or explode it into lines and/or arcs.

And now for a shape that is almost the same as a polygon.

ELLIPSE

When is a circle not a circle? When it is an ellipse. Actually, it is more correct to say the opposite: a circle is really just a special case of an ellipse—it is an ellipse that has an eccentricity of 1.

ELLIPSE works the same in all versions, but as with POLYGON the menu picks differ slightly among versions. Again I will start with the typed-in command and its options, but this time I leave it to you to figure out the menu picks. (I'll give you two hints: ELLIPSE is under {DRAW}, and LT must be showing the *full* menu.)

Two options are available for drawing an ellipse: (1) first axis and eccentricity, which is the default, or (2) center and two axes. Start ELLIPSE and try each option.

First Axis and Eccentricity

After you start ELLIPSE, AutoCAD asks you to specify Arc/Center/<Axis endpoint 1>. Axis endpoint is the default option, as indicated by the angle brackets < >.

1. Specify a point (by picking or by typing in a coordinate pair), such as P1 in Figure 10-5. Auto-CAD asks for "Axis endpoint 2."

2. Select point P2. Auto-CAD prepares to draw the ellipse about the imaginary line defined by P1 and P2. The two points will lie at opposite ends of the first axis.

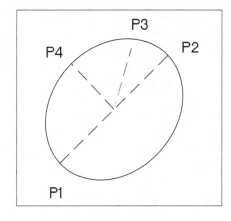

Figure 10-5: Ellipse #1

The first two points can define either the major (long) axis or the minor (short) axis, depending on what you do next.

3. AutoCAD prompts for "<Other axis distance>/Rotation." Type in a value. AutoCAD takes this value as half the length of the other axis and draws the ellipse accordingly.

   Alternately, move the cursor to "show" AutoCAD the distance. An elastic ellipse is displayed while you make up your mind as to its actual size and proportions. The significant issue here is that AutoCAD takes the distance from the cursor to the midpoint of the first axis as half the second axis's length; if you select point P3, AutoCAD draws the ellipse as though you had selected point P4. The actual ellipse will not pass through the selected point unless it is located perpendicular to the midpoint of the first axis, as shown by P4.

   The second axis can obviously end up being the major or minor axis, depending on its length relative to the first. Negative or zero axis lengths are not allowed.

4. The other option after defining the first axis is to specify the rotation of the ellipse about the major axis. To envision what this means, pick up any convenient thin, flat, circular object such as a compact disk (CD). When you look at it head on it is a circle, but as you revolve it about a diameter it appears to be an ever-narrowing ellipse. When you have revolved it 90 degrees it becomes a line.

Enter the letter R. AutoCAD prompts for the "Rotation about major axis."

▶ A value between zero and 89.4 degrees produces an ellipse that looks like you took a circle and revolved it about the first axis into the third dimension.

▶ A value of zero produces no rotation (a circle).

▶ A value of 45 degrees produces an ellipse whose minor axis is 0.707 times as long as the major axis.

▶ A value of 89.4 degrees almost produces a line.

Note that by definition the first axis will be the major axis; whenever a circle is rotated into the third dimension, the other axis must be shorter.

Center and Two Axes

Center is the second option for drawing an ellipse. Refer to Figure 10-6.

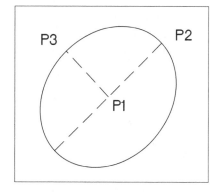

Figure 10-6: Ellipse #2

1. After you start the command, Enter C.

   AutoCAD prompts for a center point, P1. Provide one.

2. It will then ask for a point on the end of one axis (P2). Provide one.

3. Now you will be asked for a point on the end of the other axis (P3). Provide it.

The center point (P1) and the first axis endpoint (P2) define the ellipse location and the length and orientation of the first axis. The distance from the center point (P1) to the second axis point (P3) defines the length of the second axis.

As promised, I will not spell out the detailed menu picks. You should have no trouble finding them yourself.

Editing Ellipses

An ellipse in R12DOS, R12Win, and LT is quite different from an ellipse in R13Win and R13DOS.

> **R12DOS, R12Win, and LT:** Once again, there is no such *entity* as an ellipse. AutoCAD approximates one by drawing a pline composed of a whole bunch of short arc segments, in almost the same way as it creates a polygon.
>
> You can edit an ellipse in the same ways described earlier in this chapter under "Editing polygons." Rather than repeating everything I said in that section, I ask that you read and practice that section again, replacing each occurrence of a polygon with an ellipse.
>
> **R13DOS and R13Win:** These versions *do* create a mathematically-correct ellipse entity, rather than approximating one with a series of pline arcs. You can break or trim them, and you can use them as trim or to extend boundaries. You can use grip editing to change their eccentricity.
>
> They are *not* composed of pline arcs, so you cannot do those edits that apply to plines; you cannot give them width, nor can you explode them into arc segments.

DONUT

Unlike POLYGON and ELLIPSE, DONUT not only functions the same in all versions, it even has the same menu picks (once again, LT must be using the *full* menu). To use DONUT, follow these steps:

1. Pick {DRAW} {DONUT} (in R13Win, DONUT will initially be found in the flyout under CIRCLE).

   The command is simplicity itself. AutoCAD prompts for an inside diameter and defaults to showing the last one you used, enclosed in angle brackets. Provide one. Zero is legitimate as an inside diameter; it causes a filled circle to be drawn.

2. AutoCAD then prompts for an outside diameter, again defaulting to the last one you used. The outside diameter obviously must be larger than the inside diameter.

   Diameters may be typed in as specific values, or they may be "shown" by picking two points. SNAP, ORTHO, and object snap modes apply.

3. Once AutoCAD has the diameters, it asks for a center location; provide one and AutoCAD draws the appropriate ring or filled circle.

Unlike other commands, DONUT at this point does *not* drop back to the Command prompt. Instead, it keeps asking for a center location. It will plop down donuts as fast and as often as you select center points and until you terminate the command by hitting Enter, hitting Ctrl + C, or picking another command from the menu. Figure 10-7 shows a few doughnuts in a typical setting.

Figure 10-7 Doughnuts

Editing Donuts

A donut, too, is really an arc-segment pline. A pline arc must be less than 360 degrees (remember from Chapter 9?), so AutoCAD draws a donut as two 180-degree segments. The pline has a diameter that equals the mean diameter (halfway between the inside and outside diameters) and has a width equal to half the difference in the inside and outside diameters.

As expected, the material in the "Editing Polygons" section also applies to donuts. Specifically, if you use PEDIT to change the width, then the outside and inside diameters change while the mean diameter remains constant.

SKETCH

Whenever nonusers or new users see AutoCAD for the first time, they are suitably impressed by the speed and ease with which an experienced user is able to draw lines, circles, arcs, and so on. Using ORTHO and object snaps for accuracy blows them away. But invariably an early reaction is, "Very nice, but can I do freehand sketching with it?"

The answer is "Yes, but . . ."

If you really want to do freehand sketching, you should be using a graphics program such as Paintbrush rather than a drafting program like AutoCAD. However, SKETCH permits you to sketch in a freehand mode as though you were drawing with a pen or pencil. You can draw irregular shapes such as a coastline on a map or the outline of a tree. To work with SKETCH, follow these steps:

1. Start SKETCH at the Command prompt.

2. AutoCAD prompts for a record increment and offers the default of .100 units. SKETCH works by creating a series of short line segments; the "record increment" specifies the length of each of these segments and hence the coarseness or smoothness of the sketch. Hit Enter to take the default.

3. AutoCAD prompts with something like this: "Sketch. Pen eXit Quit Record Erase Connect."

   "Sketch" simply reminds you that you are in SKETCH. "Pen" refers to the "virtual pen" that creates the AutoCAD line entities. Your pointing device—mouse, joystick, or tablet puck—moves the pen around on the screen. Initially the pen is "up," which means moving the pointing device moves the pen around on the screen but no line segments are drawn yet.

4. To begin creating line segments, type P (for "Pen") or press the pick button on your pointing device. The pen then goes "down," and as the pointing device is moved it draws line segments.

   Typing P again or pressing the pick button serves as a toggle; each operation reverses the pen's status. You can thus draw several unconnected "sketched" line groups in one run of SKETCH.

As you are sketching, notice the following interesting phenomena:

▶ ORTHO is active. If ORTHO is on, all sketched line segments are perfectly horizontal or vertical. (This probably defeats the intent of sketching.)

▶ SNAP is also active. If the snap increment is larger than the record increment and SNAP is on, SNAP has priority and the ends of the sketched line segments always land on the snap points. This, too, negates the intent of sketching.

▶ Object snaps and snap overrides still work.

▶ The sketched lines appear in green on a color monitor (or red if the current color is green), regardless of the current active color.

This last item has particular significance and opens up a whole new topic for discussion.

Freehand work differs from "real" drafting, so AutoCAD provides a small set of specialized commands that are active only while you are using SKETCH.

Sketched lines do not actually become part of the drawing until you exit SKETCH or specifically instruct AutoCAD to add them. This is why they display in green (or red): they don't really exist yet. You are able to do limited editing on them before accepting them.

There are a number of subcommands available within SKETCH. I will cover just a few of the major ones. To invoke a subcommand, hit the uppercase key in column one; *do not* hit Enter or the space bar.

P   Pen. Toggles between pen up/pen down.

R   Record. Turns all the "temporary" line segments into "real" lines and records them within your drawing. It leaves the pen up or down, whichever way it found it, and returns you to sketching.

X   eXit. (You also can Enter or hit the space bar.) Records all lines and returns you to the Command prompt. (This is why you do not hit Enter or the space bar after SKETCH subcommands.)

Q   Quit. Abandons all temporary lines and returns you to the Command prompt. (Ctrl + C also quits.)

The implication is that all the sketching you have done is "free-hand," as though you were drawing directly on the display screen. If you have a digitizer tablet instead of a mouse, it is also possible to tape a paper drawing onto the digitizer tablet and then trace over it.

This is a specialized application of AutoCAD, so I will just give a brief outline of the procedure. For a meaningful tracing, you should first start TABLET to calibrate the tablet and then turn TABLET on before starting to sketch. Note that a mouse is useless for tracing because it provides information only about relative motion rather than absolute location, which is what is needed, and so cannot be calibrated.

Sketching using AutoCAD is one of those things that *can* be done but probably should *not* be done. The problem is, SKETCH generates a tremendous number of line segments in a short time. The AutoCAD manual states that "it is possible in twenty minutes of freehand sketching to create a drawing with as many lines as a normal drawing which took twenty hours to enter."

Disk space can fill up at a frighteningly fast rate, and redraw/regen times can approach geological time spans. The shorter the record increment (to get a smoother sketch), the worse things get.

And that is the good news. Try to erase a section of a sketched line by picking it (don't use a Window). Horrors! Each little segment of a sketched line is a separate, independent line. Editing the general shape of a sketched profile is so impractical as to be almost impossible. Even trying to MOVE, COPY, or MIRROR it can be an interesting exercise.

158

Nonetheless, there are still times when sketching with AutoCAD can be useful, although only as an intermediate step. If you have a complex shape you want to enter into AutoCAD, follow these steps:

1. Change to a layer that has nothing on it. Sketch your free-hand or traced profile onto this layer.

2. Change to another layer that has a different color.

3. Start PLINE, put it in Arc mode, and draw a new pline by picking suitable points along the sketched line. In this manner, several hundred short line segments can be turned into a single smooth, flowing pline with relatively few vertices which closely approximates the sketched line.

4. Change back to the layer that holds the sketch and freeze all other layers.

5. Erase everything on the sketched layer.

6. Thaw all the layers.

7. When you finish this editing session, save the drawing, then quit (rather than simply ending it) so that AutoCAD will clean out all the erased line segments from the drawing file.

Bingo! You now have a nice small drawing with "freehand" curves that are smoother than if left in their sketched state and are easier to edit. You can change the profile by using PEDIT to move a vertex, then curve-fit to smooth the curve again.

In this chapter we have covered the creation of a number of specialty entity types within AutoCAD. You will not need them very often, but when you do need them they are invaluable.

11 Crosshatching

Believe it or not, I am so old that I can remember all the way back to the lead age, when we used to use pencils and paper to do our drawings. In those days, one of the worst jobs was to hatch a cross-section. It could take hours to draw all the parallel, angled lines of a simple crosshatch pattern. A complex pattern could turn into a lifetime career.

As usual, AutoCAD's biggest labor-saving benefits come from the automation of tedious or repetitive tasks. Crosshatching certainly falls into that category.

R12DOS and R12Win introduced a new command to do crosshatching. Its operation differs quite a bit from the other versions, so I divided this chapter into two major sections: the first section covers BHATCH from R12DOS, R12Win, R13DOS, and R13Win, and the second section covers HATCH from LT. (R12DOS and R12Win still support HATCH, but the menu picks default to BHATCH.) If you are using LT or an earlier version of AutoCAD, you can jump straight to the HATCH section.

BHATCH (R12DOS, R12Win, R13DOS, and R13Win)

BHATCH gets its name from Boundary HATCH. With this command AutoCAD creates a temporary boundary line around a region you have selected and then fills the region with a cross-hatch pattern of your choice.

To see how BHATCH works, follow these steps:

1. Draw an ellipse (if you are going to hatch something, why not hatch an egg?).

2. Pick {DRAW} {HATCH...} and the Boundary Hatch dialog box appears.

3. Select a pattern. Before a wedding, the bride goes to local stores and selects a pattern for china, silverware, and so on so that when wedding guests buy these items as wedding gifts the patterns will match. AutoCAD works much the same way. Before it can crosshatch an area, it needs to know the style of crosshatch pattern you want to use. It then applies that pattern to all areas you crosshatch until you select a different pattern. The procedure for selecting a crosshatch pattern varies a little between versions.

   R12DOS and R12Win: In the dialog box, notice the upper left corner; it indicates there is no crosshatch pattern selected. Pick {Hatch Options} and a new dialog box appears. From the new dialog box, pick {Pattern . . .}. Yet another dialog box appears, showing samples of the 53 available crosshatch patterns. You can pick {Next} and {Previous} to scroll through them in sets of twelve.

   When you see something you like (I chose ANSI31 for Figure 11-1), click on its sample patch in the dialog box. The pattern box collapses and you are returned to the Hatch Options box. The name of your selected pattern now appears beside the "Pattern . . ." button. You need to select a crosshatch pattern only once per editing session, although you can change patterns as often as you want. Pick {OK} to return to the main dialog box.

   R13DOS and R13Win: The dialog box defaults to having preselected the ANSI31 pattern, which is what I used for Figure 11-1. If you want to use one of the other patterns, pick {PATTERN} from the left side of the dialog box. This will pop up a list of all available crosshatch patterns; when you select one a sample of it appears in the upper left region of the dialog box. You can keep picking different patterns until you get the one you want.

4. Apply the pattern. From the main Boundary Hatch dialog box, pick {Pick points}. AutoCAD collapses the dialog box and prompts you to "Select internal point."

5. Pick a point any-where within the ellipse, such as point P1 in the left view of Figure 11-1. Two more prompts scroll by, and Auto-CAD again prompts you to "Select inter-nal point."

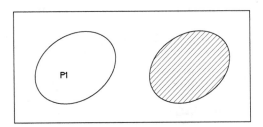

Figure 11-1: HATCH an egg

6. Hit Enter. The main dialog box reappears.

7. From the main dialog box, pick {Apply}. AutoCAD collapses the dialog box and almost instantly (depending on the speed of your machine) draws the crosshatching (see Figure 11-1).

Using Multiple Boundaries

In the previous example, you selected only one point to define a single crosshatched region. However, did you notice that Auto-CAD continued to ask for more? It doesn't restrict you to one region.

1. Draw two nested circles (of course you will draw nested cir-cles; you just hatched an egg) as shown in the left side of Figure 11-2.

2. Start BHATCH again by picking {DRAW} {HATCH}. Notice that AutoCAD now displays the name of your previously selected crosshatch pattern, so you can jump straight to the Pick Points button.

3. Pick {Pick Points}. Once again the dialog box collapses, and you are prompted to "Select internal point." The AutoCAD versions vary slightly in their operation:

R12DOS and R12Win: Pick point P1 as shown in the left view of Figure 11-2, *but* be sure to note the following:

▶ You *must* pick the point *inside* the larger circle.

▶ The point *must* be closer to the larger circle than it is to the smaller one.

AutoCAD prompts you to "Select internal point" again.

For this example, pick point P2 anywhere within the smaller circle.

R13DOS and R13Win: Pick point P1 as shown in the left view of Figure 11-2. You can ignore point P2 in this figure.

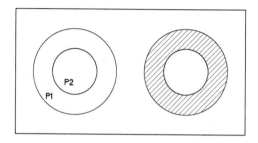

Figure 11-2: Nested Hatching

4. Enter to return to the main dialog box.

5. Pick {Apply}. AutoCAD crosshatches the space between the two circles, as shown in the right half of Figure 11-2. If you are using R13DOS or R13Win it is not necessary to pick the second point (P2 in Figure 11-2) as R12DOS or R12Win users must, because AutoCAD automatically detects the presence of the inner island within the outer boundary.

Using Multiple Crosshatchings

Nested areas need not be concentric and are not limited to one level of nesting. Figure 11-3 shows this. The two crosshatched regions were created at one time.

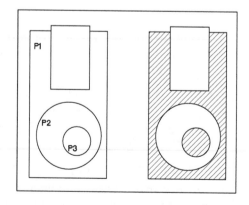

Figure 11-3: Multiple Hatching

R12DOS and R12Win: The regions to be crosshatched were defined by picking points P1, P2, and P3. Points can be picked in any order; the only requirement is that they be *inside* the desired region. This means, for example, that point P2 in the figure must be closer to the larger circle than it is to the smaller one.

To understand the location requirements for points, you must understand how BHATCH operates. When you pick a point, AutoCAD checks all entities that are currently visible on-screen. It finds the one that is closest to the picked point and then runs down the entity, looking for other entities that join, touch, or cross it. AutoCAD repeats this process until it has found enough entities or portions of them that ultimately connect back to the starting segment. This process defines the boundary.

R13DOS and R13Win: It is only necessary to select point P1 in Figure 11-3. AutoCAD will automatically detect all of the nested inner islands.

The bad news is, BHATCH has to study every visible entity to see if it helps define the boundary. The operative word in the bad news is "visible." To speed up BHATCH, you should therefore make invisible those entities that you know will not help define the boundary (nonboundary entities). You can do this by zooming in until the area to be crosshatched just fills the screen, and/or you can freeze any layers that contain nonboundary entities.

Having defined the boundary, AutoCAD then applies cross-hatching to the region surrounded by the boundary. First, however, it ensures that the original picked point is *inside* this boundary; if it isn't, AutoCAD will object by popping up a dialog box rather than trying to crosshatch the entire known universe.

Problems with Crosshatching

About all that can really go wrong when crosshatching is if AutoCAD cannot find the enclosing boundary. This is where object snaps become important; it doesn't matter if entities overlap (look at the upper rectangle in Figure 11-3), but there must not be any gaps or openings. If there is so much as a microscopic opening (to 14 decimal places), AutoCAD is unable to find the continuous enclosing boundary. In this case it usually opens a dialog box indicating that the selected point is outside the boundary. If you then pick {Look at it}, AutoCAD will put an *x* on-screen at your selected point and highlight the boundary it is analyzing.

Other Options

The Boundary Hatch dialog box has several other options, as follows:

Select objects You are not limited to picking only "internal points." If you pick {Select objects}, AutoCAD prompts you to select specific entities. This option is particularly useful if your crosshatched region includes text or dimensions. AutoCAD automatically builds a safety fence around those. If you select any text or dimension entities within your crosshatch boundary, AutoCAD does not crosshatch right over them but instead interrupts the crosshatching and leaves an unhatched area around each text or dimension entity. In R13DOS and R13Win it is not necessary to specifically select any text or dimensions within the crosshatch boundary, because AutoCAD will automatically take them into account and will not crosshatch over them.

Preview Hatch Pick {Preview Hatch} and AutoCAD displays its intended crosshatching for you to inspect. Hit Enter and the Boundary Hatch dialog box reappears. You then can either pick {Apply} to finalize the crosshatching operation or revise any options—including the pattern name, scale, and rotation angle (all of these are found in the {Hatch Options} dialog box)—and/or boundary entities.

It is thus possible to "cut and try," previewing each time until things are just right. Go ahead and practice, studying the effects of each option as you do.

Copy Existing or Inherit Properties

> **R12DOS and R12Win:** Pick {Hatch Options}, then {Copy Existing}.

> **R13DOS and R13Win:** Pick {Inherit Properties}.

AutoCAD prompts you to select an existing crosshatched region. After you do, AutoCAD reads back all the settings used to create the region and loads them in as the current values.

For example, you may have a complex assembly drawing that used several different crosshatch pattern names, scales, and rotation angles. Copy Existing or Inherit Properties allows you to jump quickly from setup to setup without having to go through the full selection process each time. It is also useful if you are editing someone else's drawing and don't know the settings they used originally.

Advanced Options Picking {Advanced Options} opens another dialog box of Options. You can ignore these for over 99 percent of your routine crosshatching. If you really want to know about these options, refer to the AutoCAD manual.

If you are not using LT, you can now skip ahead to the Editing section.

HATCH (LT)

This command works completely differently from BHATCH in R12DOS, R12Win, R13DOS, and R13Win. The net result is the same, and in fact BHATCH ultimately uses HATCH. If LT is the only AutoCAD version you have, you may want to read the BHATCH section to see what you are missing.

To see how HATCH works, follow these steps:

1. Draw an ellipse.

2. Start HATCH by picking {DRAW} {HATCH...} from the menu bar.

    A dialog box appears that displays the 53 available crosshatch patterns (pick {Next} and {Previous} to scroll through them).

3. Click on a pattern you like (I used ANSI31 for Figure 11-1). Unfortunately, you must select a pattern each time you crosshatch an area, which is a nuisance. However, if you type in HATCH at the keyboard instead of picking it from the menu, AutoCAD offers the current pattern name as the default.

AutoCAD asks for a scale for the pattern and offers the default of 1.

4. For now, just hit Enter to take the default. AutoCAD asks for an angle.

5. Hit Enter again to take the default of zero. AutoCAD prompts you to select objects.

6. All the usual selection-set mechanisms apply, including picking, Window, Crossing, and Automatic. You can use Remove and Add to build up your boundary. This time, pick the ellipse as indicated by point P1 in the left side of Figure 11-1 (be sure you pick a point somewhere on the ellipse so that it highlights).

7. When you finish selecting entities, hit Enter. AutoCAD creates the crosshatching as shown in the right side of Figure 11-1.

8. Hit Enter to have AutoCAD repeat the last command. The command repeats with a slight difference, or more specifically with a complete similarity; it assumes you want to do some more crosshatching with the same pattern at the same scale and angle.

Now try a nested structure, such as a circle within a circle as shown in the left half of Figure 11-2. Ensure your pick points P1 and P2 actually lie on the circles so that they get selected.

Hit Enter instead of selecting another entity. If you did it right, AutoCAD crosshatches the space between the circles (see the right half of Figure 11-2).

Defining Boundaries

So far, so good. The difficulty with HATCH is that the boundary of the region to be crosshatched must be defined by a single series of contiguous entities. To see what this means, look at Figure 11-4. If you want to crosshatch the central rectangle of the left half of the figure, you cannot simply pick

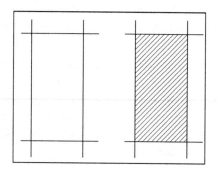

Figure 11-4: Hatch Boundary

the four lines as the boundary. You will not end up with the desired effect as shown in the right half, because the four lines do not define a series of contiguous entities—they overlap at the corners.

There are two ways to achieve the desired effect:

▶ Break each of the four lines at the four intersections, ending up with 12 line segments, and then pick the center four as the boundary.

▶ Draw a pline that passes through the four intersections. Use it as the crosshatch boundary, then erase the pline. In fact, this is what the other versions do automatically during their BHATCH command.

Crosshatch boundaries can consist of any combination of lines, circles, arcs, and polylines. The only requirement is that they *cannot* have gaps or overlaps at the corner. To ensure this, you *must* use object snaps such as END, MID, and INTersection and FILLET with a radius of zero.

Text and dimensioning are protected by an invisible fence; these entities, included in the set of boundary definition entities, are treated as if they were surrounded by this fence. Crosshatching will skip over them, leaving an unhatched area around each text or dimension entity.

Problems with HATCH

The HATCH command can be most frustrating, because the boundary entities must be perfect in order to create proper crosshatching. As indicated earlier, they must be *exactly* contiguous, with no gaps or overlaps.

A line or two missing from a crosshatching indicates that corners have a small gap or that you have missed picking a small entity (such as the radii generated by FILLET).

"Leakage," or the appearance of crosshatching in an unexpected region of the drawing, is usually caused either by overlapping corners or by several colinear line segments that appear to be a single line.

Editing Crosshatching

R12DOS, R12Win, and LT: AutoCAD does not have a mechanism for editing crosshatching. All you can do is erase the crosshatching, do any other editing, and then re-hatch the area from scratch. In **R12DOS** and **R12Win** you can use {Copy Existing} to read its settings back in as the current ones before you do the erasing.

Notice that each crosshatch behaves as one big, single entity; you can erase the entire crosshatch just by picking anywhere on it. However, this result can also be a disadvantage. Refer again to Figure 11-3. If you want to change the size of the inner circle, you first would erase the crosshatching within it. The problem is, all the crosshatching in this figure was created at one time, so if you erase the crosshatching within the small circle then *all* the crosshatching will go away. Although AutoCAD allows multiple nested crosshatching such as this figure shows, it is not always advantageous to do this. Subsequent editing is easier if each region is crosshatched separately.

R13DOS and R13Win: Crosshatch editing is greatly improved in these versions. There are two types of editing that you can do; you can change the pattern name, scale factor, and/or angle, or you can edit the entities that define the crosshatched boundary.

Editing a crosshatched region is simplicity itself. Crosshatching is associative, which means that it is connected to the boundaries that define it. If you perform any editing on any of the boundary entities, such as moving, erasing, stretching, and so on, then AutoCAD will automatically realize that the boundary has changed and will update the crosshatching to suit. This requires no action on your part. To see this in action, use grip editing to move the inner circle in Figure 11-3 and watch as the crosshatching adjusts automatically.

To edit the crosshatching itself, in R13Win pick {EDIT HATCH} from the {SPECIAL EDIT} flyout of the {MODIFY} toolbox, or in R13DOS pick {MODIFY} {EDIT HATCH}. Pick an existing crosshatched region and the original

Boundary Hatch dialog box will pop up. You can select different patterns, scale factors, and so on and can then apply the changes when you are satisfied.

General Comments on BHATCH and HATCH

Pattern Selection

More complex patterns, such as Escher and Earth, can take a long time to crosshatch and can suck up a lot of file space, especially when done at a fine scale. I once saw someone try to make wallpaper for his house by using Escher at a scale of 0.2 to fill a 34-by-96 rectangle. Four hours later, his drawing contained five entities and occupied 7 MB of file space.

AutoCAD comes with an extensive library of crosshatch patterns. If none are suitable for your purpose, refer to the AutoCAD manuals (other than that for LT), which contain complete details on how you can create custom patterns. Other sources of custom patterns are the advertisers and "tips" sections in independent AutoCAD magazines such as *CADalyst, AutoCAD User,* and *CADENCE,* as well as from user groups, computer bulletin boards, and CompuServe.

Scale Factor

The standard AutoCAD crosshatch patterns have a characteristic size of one drawing unit. In Chapter 13 I will cover the general topic of scale factors for drawings. Suffice it to say for now that if you are working with scales that are significantly different from unity then you will have trouble with your crosshatch patterns. In the short term you can experiment with scale factors in the range of 0.5 for a fine pattern to about 2.0 for a coarse pattern. This is commonly done to differentiate between different components in a cutaway or sectioned assembly drawing, for example.

Rotation Angle

The correct rotation angles are normally built into the patterns, so if you are using, for example, ANSI31, which produces lines at a 45-degree angle, you would leave the rotation angle at zero. If you want to differentiate between two adjacent crosshatched areas, you can specify an angle of 90 degrees for one of them.

Doing this produces crosshatching that goes "uphill" to the left instead of to the right.

As I have done with other subjects in this book, I have not taught you all there is to know about crosshatching. However, what I have covered will account for over 90 percent of your usage.

12 Blocks and Attributes

The AutoCAD manual describes a *block* as "a set of entities grouped together into a compound object." What this really means is that you can draw an object (a toilet, for example) and then link its parts together to form a block that AutoCAD considers to be a single entity. If you then start ERASE and point to a single line within a block, the entire block will be erased. You can put another toilet in the drawing simply by inserting it, rather than by redrawing each of its separate entities.

Why Use Blocks?

The obvious question is, "Why bother? Why not just use COPY?" Well, there are several good answers to that question, as follows.

They Save Space

Using COPY to replicate many copies of a repeated detail within a drawing is very inefficient. Each copy of the detail increases the drawing file size by the total space required for the sum of all the entities within the detail. A block insertion, on the other hand, defines the detail only once, so each insertion requires only a small amount of space.

For example, say I had a drawing that took up 40K of disk space. When I made a ten-by-ten array of everything in the drawing—

which effectively copied it one hundred times—and saved it, the disk file jumped to 4,000K, or 100 times the original. On the other hand, when I made a block of everything in the original drawing, arrayed it ten by ten—which effectively inserted it one hundred times—and saved it, the resulting file was only 43K.

They Save Work

When you use BLOCK, you need draw a detail only once. A complicated drawing can be easily constructed in a building-block fashion using blocks.

AutoCAD is brilliant in its approach to blocks. It allows any existing drawing to be inserted into any other drawing with no special command or preparation. It is not necessary to redraw and redefine a standard detail for every new drawing; just make one drawing of the detail, save it to disk, and insert it into the new drawing. You can use this feature to build a library of standard details, each drawn by itself as a normal drawing that can then be inserted where needed. Many manufacturers now offer their catalogs on disk as AutoCAD drawings, ready to roll into your drawing.

They Make Editing Easy

Suppose you are just putting the finishing touches on the plans for a 4,200-room hotel and then realize that you have included the wrong toilet. There is no need to flush your drawings down the sewer; simply redefine your toilet block and all toilets everywhere in the drawing will be updated automatically.

They Make Assigning Attributes Easy

Blocks can have tags hung on them that contain information that varies with each insertion. These tags serve two purposes. They make it much easier to display information about the item, such as the value and part number of a resistor on a printed circuit board. Also, this information can be extracted and passed to other programs, such as database managers and spreadsheets.

Now that you understand the benefits of blocks, it is time to jump in and try a few examples.

BLOCK

BLOCK is used in the current drawing to link up selected entities into a single "super entity"—a block. To create a block, follow these steps:

1. Start a new drawing and create a few entities in it like those in Figure 12-1. (Ignore the P1 for now; I will refer to it shortly.)

2. Start BLOCK. How you do this varies by version. You can always enter it at the Command prompt, or you can pick it as follows:

    R12DOS, R12Win and R13DOS: Pick {CONSTRUCT} {BLOCK} from the menu bar.

    LT: Pick {CONSTRUCT} {MAKE BLOCK} from the *full* menu.

    Figure 12-1: Tree

    R13Win: Pick {BLOCK} from the {DRAW} toolbox.

    Once started, BLOCK works the same way in all versions. AutoCAD asks for a "Block name."

3. Enter a block name. Names can be up to 31 characters long and may contain letters, numbers, dollar signs ($), hyphens (-), and underscores (_). Note that AutoCAD converts all characters in block names to uppercase, so toilet, TOILET, and ToiLEt are all the same name. A suitable name for your current block might be Tree.

    AutoCAD prompts for an "Insertion base point." This is the point on the block that will be the selected point during subsequent insertions of the block. It also is the point around which the block can be rotated and/or scaled during insertion.

4. Enter the insertion base point. It is good practice to use an object-snap mode to pick a logical insertion point (such as the center of a circular detail within the block, the end or middle of a line, or the intersection of two entities). If you know a different logical location, you can also use the keyboard to type in an exact coordinate. I suggest that in this exercise you use point P1, as shown in Figure 12-1.

AutoCAD prompts you to "Select objects."

5. You can select any type of entity, including lines, circles, text, and even other blocks, using any of the standard entity selection methods, including picking, Window, Crossing, Previous, and Last. Many CAD systems do not allow nesting of blocks, but AutoCAD not only allows it, it places no restriction on the depths to which you nest ("bigger fleas have smaller fleas . . ." and so on). You can also toggle between Add and Remove until you get the desired set; for example, you could Window a set of entities and then remove the temporary line that was used to define the base point.

6. After you have selected the objects, hit Enter to complete the command.

   Hey, where did everything go? In all versions except LT, AutoCAD erases all the selected entities from the drawing and transfers them to the block definition. If you still need the entities in the original location, you will need to insert the block at that location (using your "base point" construction line?) so that it becomes the first block reference instead of a collection of loose entities.

   LT does not erase the entities, but it is usually good practice to erase them yourself (by using Erase Previous) so you do not end up with a duplicate set—the entities, and the block definition.

Repeat BLOCK, and when AutoCAD prompts for a block name, reply with a ?. AutoCAD responds with a list of all blocks contained within the drawing. "Unnamed" blocks are blocks that AutoCAD created itself, such as sections of cross-hatching or "associative dimensions."

INSERT

With INSERT you can place copies of a block into your drawing. This command works as follows:

1. Start the command by picking {DRAW} {INSERT}. A dialog box appears.

2. Pick {BLOCK}. AutoCAD brings up a list of all blocks currently defined in your drawing.

3. Double-click on Tree to select the name of your block, then pick {OK}. AutoCAD prompts for an insertion point. This point is the same as the insertion base point you specified when you created the block.

4. You can type in or point to a location and use all the regular snap modes such as CENter, END, and MIDdle. AutoCAD displays a ghost image of your block that you can drag around to see how it will fit before you select the insertion point. After you select an insertion point, AutoCAD prompts for an X-scale factor.

5. Either Enter for 1.0 or type in a number. AutoCAD asks for a Y-scale factor, whose default is the value of the X factor.

6. Hit Enter to accept the default or type in a number. Note that negative scale factors are legal and produce a mirror image. You can also use your pointing device to "show" AutoCAD the X and Y factors simultaneously, although doing this can be tricky.

   AutoCAD prompts for a rotation angle.

7. Either hit Enter to default to zero, type in the number of degrees you want, or use your pointing device to "show" AutoCAD the angle.

8. Having "planted a tree," hit Enter to repeat the last command. AutoCAD "remembers" the name of the last block you inserted and offers it as the default.

9. Hit Enter to accept the default.

Repeat these steps several times, experimenting with different scale factors and rotation angles, until you have grown a "forest" that resembles Figure 12-2.

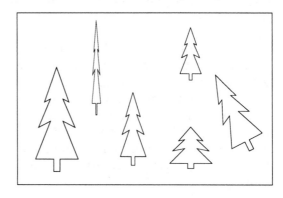

Figure 12-2: Forest

An inserted block to some degree takes on the properties of the layer that is current when it is inserted. The block will exist on the current layer. Any entities within the block definition that have layer, color, and/or line type specifications will retain them, *except* anything on layer 0 (zero), which will take on the properties of the layer on which the block is inserted.

Inserting Another Drawing

With INSERT you can insert any other drawing from disk into the current drawing. A copy of the other drawing then becomes a block definition within the current drawing. *Any* drawing can be inserted into any other without any special preparation. This is how you make use of your library of standard detail drawings, including the manufacturer's catalogs that were mentioned earlier in this chapter. Follow these steps:

1. Start INSERT by picking {DRAW} {INSERT}. A dialog box appears.

2. Pick {FILE}. AutoCAD brings up a list of all drawings in the current directory. You can also browse through all other directories and drives by clicking on the appropriate boxes.

3. Select the drawing you want to insert. AutoCAD returns you to the normal prompts for insertion point, scale factor, and rotation angle.

Where is the insertion base point on a drawing being inserted from disk? Usually it is point 0,0. However, if you edit the drawing you can use BASE to specify any point as the insertion base point.

If the incoming drawing already contains block definitions, they are added to the current drawing. If any incoming block definition has the same name as an existing one in the current drawing, the current drawing's definition has precedence, and the incoming definition is ignored. Any insertions of it in the incoming drawing will take on the existing definition in the current drawing. Any new layers, line types, text styles, and so on from the incoming drawing are automatically added to the current drawing.

Editing Blocks

Suppose you decide you need to change the forest to a different type of tree. No problem! Draw the new tree as shown in Figure 12-3, then follow these steps:

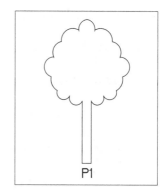

Figure 12-3: New Tree

1. Start BLOCK again.

2. When AutoCAD asks for a name, enter Tree. AutoCAD reminds you that block Tree already exists and asks if you want to redefine it.

3. Reply, "Yes." BLOCK behaves exactly as it did earlier, prompting you to provide an insertion point (P1 in Figure 12-3) and select entities. After you select all your entities, the selected set disappears, as usual. AutoCAD then regenerates the drawing. All your existing trees take on the new shape, as shown in Figure 12-4, although they retain the scale factors and rotation angles from their original insertions.

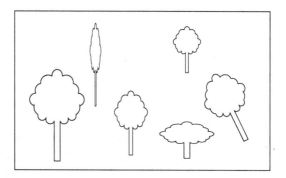

Figure 12-4: New Forest

You also can edit blocks using INSERT directly (by typing it in directly at the Command prompt) instead of using the dialog box. When you name the block, AutoCAD typically looks for the block first in the drawing. If you add an equals sign (=) after the block name, AutoCAD instead looks on the disk first.

This method can also be used to redefine an existing block. Suppose you had a drawing on disk called TREE. Inserting TREE= would tell AutoCAD to go directly to disk, bring in the TREE drawing, and use it to redefine the TREE block in the current drawing.

Yet another method to redefine a block is to add a different name after the equals sign, as in FRAMMLSTAT=WIDGET. This would redefine the block Frammlstat in your drawing to be identical to the drawing Widget on disk. This technique is helpful when working on drawings—especially architectural ones—that can get very large and hence are slow to redraw and regen. A common trick is to use a simple block definition to represent a complex block. Once the drawing is completed, and just before the final plot, redefine the block to be equal to a more complex one on disk. Every insertion of that block within your drawing updates to the more detailed representation.

EXPLODE

EXPLODE "blows up" a block insertion, turning it into loose entities again, but with certain restrictions: in R12DOS, R12Win, and LT the X- and Y-scale factors must be equal and positive, and the block cannot have been mirrored after insertion. R13DOS and R13Win do not have these restrictions.

The size of your drawing file increases by the addition of all the new entities, because the original block definition still remains in the drawing, even if you exploded the last insertion of it.

To find EXPLODE:

> **R12DOS, R12Win, and R13DOS:** Look under {MODIFY} in the menu bar.
>
> **LT:** Look under {MODIFY} in the *full* menu.
>
> **R13Win:** Look for the firecracker icon in the {MODIFY} toolbox.

By the way, this command will also explode a pline into separate line and arc entities.

*INSERT

This is not a separate command, but rather a different way of using the standard one. It is pronounced "star insert."

If you add an asterisk (*) in front of the block name as you insert a block, for example *TREE, the block comes in as its loose pieces, not as a block. This result is the same as if you had done a regular insert and then exploded it. You can also get this effect by picking the Explode button in the Insert dialog box.

This function can be most useful when you want to revise a block definition. Just insert the block with the asterisk before the name, make the changes, then block it again. Note that there is only one prompt for scale during an *INSERT operation, as the X factor must equal the Y.

This is also the best way to insert another drawing when what you really want is to end up with just a portion of the incoming drawing. For example, suppose you are currently editing a 100K drawing file and you want only 10K of another 100K drawing. If you insert the second drawing into the current drawing, your current drawing becomes 200K. Now explode the recent arrival. Your drawing grows to 300K! All you wanted was 10K of the incoming drawing, but even if you erase everything you don't want, you will still end up with a 210K drawing. On the other hand, if you insert the second drawing with an asterisk in front of its name, it comes in already exploded. Your drawing grows to 200K, but you then erase 90K of it so that you end up with only a 110K drawing file.

WriteBLOCK

WBLOCK (WriteBLOCK) copies a block out of your drawing to a disk file. That file then becomes a standard drawing and can be edited or inserted like any other drawing. This is a useful function for making a set of component drawings from a single assembly layout. To work with this command, follow these steps:

1. Start WBLOCK by entering it from the Command prompt. AutoCAD prompts for a file name.

2. Name the new file. AutoCAD prompts for a block name.

3. Enter the name of an existing block or of a new block (one that has not been defined).

If you enter the name of an existing block, AutoCAD simply copies it out to disk, where it becomes a drawing in its own right. On the other hand, the block need not already be defined in the current drawing. If you give the name of a block that does not exist in the current drawing, AutoCAD drops into what appears to be the normal BLOCK command and lets you define the block "on the fly." You will be prompted to provide a base point and to select entities, after which the entities will disappear from your drawing as usual. You can use OOPS! or UNDO to bring them back.

There is one common misconception about WBLOCK. Many beginners think the only way you can insert a drawing from disk is to use WBLOCK on it first. As you have already seen, this is not true; *any* existing drawing can be inserted without any special effort. WBLOCK exists solely to let you copy part of an existing drawing out to disk so you can make a separate drawing of it. Once the command is finished, AutoCAD has no way of knowing that you did not draw it from scratch.

XREF

AutoCAD has another mechanism for inserting information from one drawing into another—XREF, which stands for "eXternal REFerence." It works like BLOCK except that the block definition does not live within the current drawing. All the current drawing holds is the name of the other drawing. When you open a drawing that contains XREFs, AutoCAD goes back out to disk and loads in the *current* version of the externally referenced drawing.

This is one of those good news/bad news things. Your current drawing is a lot smaller and always displays the latest version of the block, but the XREF files must be present on disk whenever you open a master drawing.

XREFs are a bit of a specialty item; they do not apply to every drawing, but where they do apply, they are indispensable. The AutoCAD manual contains full details about them.

Attributes

Most articles on attributes are a little intimidating in that they very quickly lead straight into a discussion of attribute extraction and the transfer of data into Lotus or dBASE. Even the AutoCAD manual, by the third sentence of its introduction to the subject, refers to "processing by an application such as a bill-of-materials program."

Actually, attributes are extremely easy to use. They are a powerful form of customizing, even if you never extract anything back out to be processed elsewhere.

An attribute is really just a special type of entity that has text associated with it. Coincidentally, the text can be pulled out of the drawing and used by other programs, but you don't need to worry about that to make good use of attributes. I prefer to think of an attribute as a "fill-in-the-blank" entity.

It is quite common to insert a block of a standard detail, then return later and use TEXT to write a unique label beside it. By using attributes, you can do this all in one hit.

The basic procedure consists of three steps:

1. Create an attribute. This involves defining the blank to be filled in, including such parameters as the location, size, and style of the text to be used.

2. Create a block and include the attribute as one of its entities.

3. Insert the block. AutoCAD prompts not only for the usual block insertion parameters—location, scale factors, and rotation angle—but also for the fill-in-the-blank data. It then inserts the block and the text you gave it, using the text parameters you used when you defined the attribute (see step 1).

Suppose you had to draw an organization chart for a large company. This usually would involve drawing many little boxes and then putting someone's name in each box. However, you have probably already realized that you could simplify things by drawing one box, making a block of it, inserting it all over your chart, and putting a line of text in each box.

With attributes, this process becomes even simpler.

Defining Attributes

First, define the attributes as follows:

1. Start ATTDEF (ATTribute DEFinition) by typing it at the Command prompt. AutoCAD returns a cryptic prompt pertaining to attribute modes.

2. For now, hit Enter to take the default (in fact, this is your best choice most of the time). AutoCAD asks for an attribute tag, which is what it uses to identify each attribute later.

3. For this exercise, type in NAME and Enter. You can use any name you want, provided it contains no spaces. AutoCAD will also convert it to all uppercase.

   AutoCAD asks for an "Attribute prompt." Later, during block insertion, AutoCAD will display this prompt while it is waiting for you to enter data.

4. Type in "Please enter a name: " and hit Enter. AutoCAD asks for a "Default Attribute value."

5. Type in "Fred" and hit Enter. ATTDEF drops into something that looks suspiciously like TEXT.

6. You can use any previously defined style and/or any of the alignment modes. Specify centered justification, an insertion point, a size (if your style doesn't already include one), and a rotation angle.

   ATTDEF does not ask for any text. Instead it automatically plugs in the attribute tag you gave it earlier (NAME) and places it on the screen.

Defining the Block

Next, you define the block.

7. Use LINE to draw a box around NAME (see Figure 12-5).

Figure 12-5: Name tag

8. Start BLOCK and create a block called NAME-TAG. Give it a suitable insertion point. AutoCAD prompts you to select the entities.

9. Pick all the border lines *and the attribute.* You can use the Window mode to simply select everything. Note that an attribute is an entity in its own right. A block need not contain any other entities besides an attribute.

Inserting the Block

10. Use INSERT to insert your new block nametag. AutoCAD responds with all the standard prompts for insertion point, scale factors, and rotation angle. In addition, you get one more prompt, asking you to "Please enter a name:." (Does that prompt sound familiar? You supplied it as part of the attribute definition.)

11. Type in "Sue" and hit Enter. AutoCAD inserts a box with the name Sue written in the middle of it.

12. Use INSERT to insert the same block several more times, replying with a different name each time.

Now, isn't that much faster and easier than drawing each box separately and then using TEXT to write in each name? The entire chart in Figure 12-6 took me less than five minutes. Not only that, the text is automatically centered in the

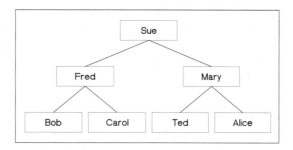

Figure 12-6: Organization Chart

box each time and uses the style specified in the attribute definition, no matter what style may now be current (or it uses Standard if you didn't specify a style). What happens if you just hit Enter instead of filling in a name when requested? That's right, AutoCAD uses the default value, "Fred," that you specified in the definition.

Now we will take a closer look at some of the details I lightly skipped over earlier.

Multiple Attributes

There is no law saying that you can have only one attribute per block. You could define a block called DOOR that has multiple attributes listing the door size, brand, model, hinges, lock set, deadbolt, fire rating, and so on.

As you know, if you hit Enter at the Command prompt, AutoCAD repeats the last command. Also, if you hit Enter after completing a TEXT command, AutoCAD assumes you want another line of text aligned below the preceding one, using the same style and alignment, so it prompts only for the additional text. ATTDEF combines these two functions. Hit Enter after you finish using ATTDEF, and AutoCAD assumes you want to define another attribute below the preceding one, using all the same text definition parameters. Recall from the note above that you can have a block that contains only several aligned attributes. Upon insertion, you would be prompted for all the values. An aligned bunch of text would then appear in your drawing.

Attribute Modes

Invisible Invisible mode enables you to specify that attributes be invisible. Their values will not be displayed or plotted, but they are available for later extraction and manipulation. This can be handy if you have quite a few attributes attached to one block, which could become too cluttered in the drawing. ATTDISP displays invisible information.

Constant Constant mode doesn't prompt for a value, but always inserts a predefined constant value. This value cannot be changed later, so at first glance it would not seem to be much different from a simple line of text included in the block. However, it is an attribute value that can be extracted for later analysis and so could be used, for example, to give a count of all doors in a building.

Verify Verify mode lets you type in a value, then asks if it is OK. If it isn't, you can correct it. This sounds like a good idea, but the extra keystrokes to correct can be a little frustrating.

Editing Attributes

Several editing operations can be performed on attributes. By far the most common is to change the text value of a single insertion; for example, in the example earlier in this chapter, Fred retires and is replaced by George.

DDATTE

DDATTE prompts you to select a block. A dialog box then appears that shows the tag and the current value of any attached attributes. Just click on the desired box or boxes, change the text, pick {OK}, and presto, the attributes are updated.

ATTEDIT

ATTEDIT is extremely powerful and versatile; for example, you can do a search and replace by attribute tag, value, substring within values, and so on. A full description of it is beyond the scope of this book.

Redefining Attributes

What if you want to change the basic definition? The AutoCAD manual makes passing reference to the fact that you can use CHANGE to change attribute definitions, however, the attribute must be unconnected (that is, not part of a block yet). To change the definition of an attribute associated with a block, you must first explode the block, or else insert it with an asterisk in front of the block name. Now CHANGE will let you change almost all the attribute's parameters, including the tag, prompt, default, and all the text parameters (*except* alignment). You can then re-define the block using the new attribute definition.

There is one significant point the AutoCAD manual overlooks regarding redefining attributes. Usually if you create a block and reuse the name of an existing block, the drawing regens and all prior insertions of the block are globally updated to the new definition. But this is the crunchy bit: this does *not* apply to any attributes that were associated with those block insertions. Those attributes still retain the original definition for text style, size, alignment, and so on. Any new insertions of the block will use the new attribute definition, but existing ones will not be updated.

EXPLODE

If you explode a block that has attributes attached, all attribute values are lost. The value displayed on-screen disappears and is replaced by the attribute's tag, just as if this were a new attribute definition being created for the first time. In fact, it can simply be reused as is in any new block creation.

In spite of their power, attributes are very easy to use. As usual, some of the simplest solutions are the most elegant. For example, I do not like fractions to be all in line and the same size as the integer (as in 1¾), so I created a block called FRAC. It consists of a single horizontal line with an attribute tagged NUMERATOR above and one called DENOMINATOR below. Both attributes use a small text style (.090 units high) and centered alignment. Now whenever I want a fraction, I just insert the block called FRAC, reply with the numerator and denominator when prompted, and hey, presto, I have a perfect vertically aligned fraction.

13 Drawing Scales, Inquiry Commands, and Units

It may seem strange to lump together the three subjects covered by this chapter, but by the end of the chapter I think you will see the connection.

Drawing Scales

In traditional drafting, the scale was the ratio between the size of the real object and the size of its drawing. In AutoCAD, however, we always draw everything *full size*.

That's right, full size. In the good old days of pencil-and-paper drafting, we had a drawer containing a selection of standard paper sizes. The first thing we did when starting a new drawing was to study the object to be drawn and the drawer full of standard paper. We would then pick a scale factor and a sheet size such that our drawing would just fit. However, text and dimensioning were always drawn the same size, usually ⅛ inch high. Similarly, noncontinuous line types and cross-hatching were always drawn to the same proportions. Consequently, many is the drawing that had to be started over because the incorrect scale factor was chosen or because the object to be drawn changed size during the design process.

With AutoCAD, however, we do it the other way around. We always draw all objects full size, so that one object unit equals one drawing unit. It doesn't matter if we are drawing an atom or a map of the known universe.

We can elect to have 1 drawing unit represent 1 inch, 1 mile, 1 furlong, 1 Angstrom, or whatever, as long as 1 equals 1. Thus a building 50 feet long would normally be drawn $50 \times 12 = 600$ units (inches) long. A tumbler pin for a lock cylinder that is .115 inches in diameter would be drawn .115 units across, and a map of North America would be drawn 5,600 units (kilometers) wide. Recall that in Chapter 2 I referred to a drawing of the known universe that is 6×10^{22} meters across.

UNITS, covered later in this chapter, allows you to select foot and inch measurements, but this really means that one unit is still 1 inch. AutoCAD simply breaks up any dimensioning or other measurements into 12-unit clumps for convenience.

You should be consistent within an office or a discipline; do not use 1 unit to represent one centimeter if the person at the next desk is using 1 unit to equal 1 millimeter on the same project.

Why do it this way? Well, mainly because it works, for the following reasons:

▶ If all drawings are done at 1 = 1, you do not have to do any arithmetic to convert distances as you draw.

▶ The program does all the work during dimensioning. If 1 = 1, AutoCAD computes the correct number automatically, with no further conversion needed.

▶ If all drawings are done to consistent units, assemblies and overlays can easily be built simply by inserting component items into a master drawing.

Now that you have finished drawing the object, it is time to plot it.

"Great," you say. "I did a map of the known universe full-size like you said. Assuming I can find a piece of paper that big, who is going to help me fold it?"

No, no, that's not the way it works. When you plot, you tell PLOT to scale the drawing down or up as appropriate to make it fit the available paper. You can do this either by telling AutoCAD to plot to fit the selected paper size or by setting the "plotted units = drawing units" factors to get an exact scale.

With AutoCAD's plotter units set to millimeters, the map may be plotted at 1 plotted unit = 25 drawing units; the 5,600-kilometer map would reduce to 224 millimeters on paper.

Similarly, the 50-foot building could be plotted at 1 = 48 to yield a 12½-inch image on C-size paper. Why 48? Because $4 \times 12 = 48$, so this is really ¼ inch to the foot.

Conversely, the .115-inch lock part would be plotted at 10 = 1, so it ends up enlarged to 1.15 inches on A-size paper.

So far, so good. Now comes one or two other details that are the reverse of traditional thinking.

I just said that you are going to scale things when you plot, but don't forget that AutoCAD will scale *everything*, including text, dimensions, hatch patterns, and noncontinuous-line type patterns. If you were to label your building drawing with ⅛-inch text and then divide by 48 when you plot, the text would end up 0.0026 inch high on paper. Old people like me are going to have some trouble reading text this fine. You had better draw the text a little larger in AutoCAD so it comes out a reasonable size on paper.

So how much is a little larger? Well, I said that you should have AutoCAD divide by 48 when it plots, so you had better make your text 48 times larger in the drawing to make it come out the right size on paper. Thus text that is 6 units high will plot out at 6 divided by 48, or 0.125 inch tall, on paper.

Conversely, the .115-inch lock part would need text that is only .0115 units tall, because you are going to enlarge it ten times when you plot.

You can specify an appropriate text size every time you enter some text, but it is easier to use STYLE. You can redefine the Standard style to have a fixed height (other than zero), and all subsequent text and dimensioning will be created at the correct height. If you have other text styles defined, they can be set accordingly.

These same factors hold true for hatch patterns, noncontinuous-line types, and the component parts of dimensions such as arrowheads and extension line gaps. These factors are controlled by issuing the commands HPSCALE, LTSCALE, and DIMSCALE to set these three factors as required.

LTSCALE and DIMSCALE settings are saved with the drawing and so will "stick" between editing sessions. Unfortunately, HPSCALE doesn't do the same. You can reset it by issuing HPSCALE directly or simply by starting HATCH or BHATCH and specifying a scale. This scale will stick for the rest of the current editing session.

The bottom line is that you do not need to consider your drawing scale until it is time to add text, dimensioning, and hatching. LTSCALE can be set at any time and will retroactively change all noncontinuous lines in the drawing, but any change to text style sizes, DIMSCALE, and HPSCALE will apply only to objects created after they are set. However, the final plotting scale *must* be decided before you add text, dimensioning, and hatching, because if you change your mind later all you can do is erase and redo them.

To help you out, here are a few useful values that will cover the typical range of drawing scales. You should be able to easily extend them to other scale factors and text sizes.

SCALE	⅛" TEXT	LTSCALE, DIMSCALE, HPSCALE
⅛"=1'	12	96
¼"=1'	6	48
½"=1'	3	24
¼ size	.5	4
full size	.125	1
2×	.0625	.5
5×	.025	.2
10×	.0125	.1
20×	.00625	.05

One other factor does not have to be set, but it is nice to do so. AutoCAD generally works faster if the limits are set to be about the same as the extents of your drawing. You should thus set them to be equal to the nominal paper size, multiplied by the LTSCALE factor. A drawing that is ¼ inch = 1 foot on C-size paper at 22×17 inch would thus have limits of 0,0 and 1056,816, which equal 48 times 22 and 17, respectively.

Here are two final thoughts:

▶ SCALE is used to shrink or magnify objects within your drawing and has nothing to do with setting scale factors.

▶ You may hear about something in AutoCAD called "paper space." In theory paper space should take care of all your text scaling. You should be able to draw your objects at full size in model space and then create model viewports in paper space to look at them. You should be able to zoom in or zoom out to set the correct apparent scale factor between the model space and paper space. All text and dimensioning would be done full size in paper space, and all drawings would be plotted at 1 = 1.

In practice, however, there are still a few problems with this concept.

For one, associative dimensioning does not link across the space boundaries, so stretching the object in model space will not change its dimension in paper space. Also, when you are in paper space AutoCAD forces a regen every time you pan or zoom, no matter by how little.

Inquiry Commands

AutoCAD has several inquiry commands available that provide a variety of information about your drawing. The easy way to find these commands is to pick the indicated menu bar item(s) as follows:

R12DOS, R12Win, and R13DOS: Pick {ASSIST} {INQUIRY}.

LT: Pick {ASSIST}.

Next, pick the appropriate command from the pop-down menu that appears.

R13Win: Pick {TOOLS} {TOOLBARS} {OBJECT PROPERTIES}, then pick them from the {INQUIRY} flyout.

These commands are discussed in the following sections.

LIST

Probably the most used of the inquiry commands, LIST tells you all about a selected item or items. Pick LIST, and AutoCAD prompts you to select entities (the usual selection-set mechanisms apply). After you do so, LIST tells you all about a selected item, including the layer on which it lives and its color and line type if they differ from those specified for the layer. Try listing a line, circle, arc, pline, dimension, block insertion, and some text to see the different information you get. LIST provides the start and end point of a line; the center, radius, circumference, and area of a circle; each vertex of a pline as well as its total length and the area it surrounds; and so on as appropriate for each entity type.

DISTance

DISTance is probably the next most commonly used inquiry command. It prompts you to select two points. After you do so, it tells you the horizontal, vertical, and net distances between the two points and the angle from the horizontal. (Note that running object snaps, SNAP, ORTHO, and snap overrides all apply.)

STATUS

STATUS tells you rather more than you may want to know about your drawing and about how AutoCAD is currently operating. It is not available in LT. It shows the number of entities in your drawing; the current limits, extent, layer name; the color and line type of the current layer; OSNAP modes; GRID and SNAP settings and status; and so on.

R12DOS, R13DOS, and R13Win also show memory (RAM) usage in your computer. In particular, you can check

▶ WhetherAutoCAD is finding all available memory in your system. Its "Total conventional memory" listing plus its "Total extended memory" value, plus any allocation for DOS's "Smartdrv" if it is running, usually should come close to matching the total memory in your system. If it does not, something may be wrong with your computer's configuration.

▶ How much memory AutoCAD would like to have. This information follows the "Virtual memory allocated to program" message and starts at about 2,000K for R12DOS, and 4,000K for R13DOS and R13Win. This amount will grow depending on how big your drawing is, how much editing you have done to it, and which add-ins, such as Render and the solid modeler, you are using. If the "Virtual memory allocated to program" exceeds the "Total extended memory," AutoCAD overflows to disk. AutoCAD then slows down considerably, and your hard drive will thrash noisily. If this happens regularly, your system would run considerably faster if it had more memory.

AREA

AREA indicates the area and perimeter length of a region. It operates in several different modes, as follows:

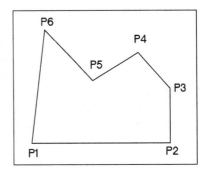

Figure 13-1: AREA Boundary

Picked Points

The default mode, picked points prompts you to indicate the boundaries of a region. After you have done so, it gives the area enclosed and the perimeter.

However, you cannot just point to existing lines; you must trace out the area again, point by point (for example, as indicated by points P1 to P6 in Figure 13-1). Object snaps, especially END, are essential in order to get an accurate reading on an existing figure. Setting running OSNAPs of END and INT will save a lot of effort.

Enter when you are ready for the result (the defined perimeter need not close back to the start; AutoCAD will make the connection for you). The bad news is that arcs can only be approximated with straight line sections.

Entity

Start AREA, then enter an E for Entity. You are prompted to select a circle or a pline entity. AREA then displays the perimeter and enclosed area of the selected entity.

A pline can be as complex as you want. It can even be splined or curve-fitted. If it doesn't close back to the start, AutoCAD, when calculating the area, creates a temporary imaginary segment and assumes it does close.

Plines can contain arc segments. An easy way to find the area of a complex region is to use PEDIT to join the boundary into a single pline and then find its area.

Note that any width information is ignored; AREA assumes a pline has zero width.

Add

If you enter an A *before* picking a point or entering an E, AREA flips into Add mode. This mode offers two options: picking points or changing to Entity mode. After you pick points or select an entity, AREA displays the area and perimeter but does not drop back to the Command prompt afterward. Instead it lets you keep on picking points or entities. With each selection, it adds the current value to the preceding one and displays a running total.

Subtract

Subtract mode is available only when you are in Add mode. It behaves the same as Add does, except it subtracts the current value from the running total. You can flip back and forth as desired between Add and Subtract, so you could find, for example, the total area and shoreline of the seven seas by adding each one and subtracting the islands.

You can add or subtract only the full area of a circle from the running total; you cannot find the area of a crescent by subtracting overlapping circles.

BPOLY

BPOLY (Boundary POLYline) works similarly to HATCH. It is available in R12DOS, R12Win, R13DOS, and R13Win only.

Recall that BHATCH creates a temporary pline around a region to be cross-hatched. You then pick a point within the region, after which AutoCAD cross-hatches the region and erases the pline.

BPOLY uses the same mechanism as BHATCH to produce the boundary polyline. You then can use AREA to find the area enclosed by the pline. BPOLY does not erase the pline when it is finished. You must use ERASE and do it yourself.

UNITS

So far I have made virtually no reference to units of measure in AutoCAD. Early in this chapter I stressed the importance of drawing everything full size, with 1 drawing unit equal to 1 of whatever unit you are working with. That is true as far as it goes. However, to help you use certain measuring systems, AutoCAD gives you five different formats for displaying linear measurements, plus five different formats for displaying angular measurements. In addition, angles can be measured clockwise or counterclockwise, and angles can start measuring from any one of the four principle directions. This gives a grand total of two hundred possible formats! How you access these formats varies by version.

> **R12DOS and R12Win:** Pick {SETTINGS} {UNITS CONTROL}. A dialog box appears.

> **LT:** Pick {SETTINGS} {UNITS STYLE} from the *full* menu. A dialog box appears.

> **R13DOS, R13Win:** Pick {DATA} {UNITS}. A dialog box appears.

The following should explain what each section of the dialog box does.

Linear Units

Scientific Displays units as a number with one digit to the left of the decimal. To the right are several numbers, the letter E, a plus or minus sign, and a number for the exponent (power of 10) to which the number is raised. An example is 1.2374E+6, which is equal to 1,237,400. This format is most useful when you are dealing with very large or very small numbers.

Decimal Displays units as simple decimal numbers. This format is most useful when you are dealing with metric units or using whole inches and decimals of inches, such as when designing doorknob parts or similar mechanical components.

Engineering One of two formats that deal in a specific measuring system. In this mode, 1 drawing unit equals 1 inch and distances are displayed in feet, inches, and decimal representations of an inch. For example, 15½ inches would be displayed as 1'-3.5".

Architectural This is the other format that assumes 1 drawing unit equals 1 inch. In this mode units are displayed in feet, inches, and fractions of an inch. For example, 15½ inches would be displayed as 1'-3½".

Fractional Displays values as whole numbers and fractions. In this case, 15½ inches would display as 15½.

Having selected the coordinate format you can then specify the desired decimal place, or denominator of smallest fraction, as appropriate. You can display fractions to the nearest ½₅₆.

Angular Units

For example:

▶ Decimal degrees: 45.00

▶ Degrees/minutes/seconds: 45d0'0"

▶ Grads: 50.00g

▶   Radians: 0.785r

▶   Surveyor: N45d0'0"E

You can also specify the precision of angular display, the direction for angle 0 (zero), and whether angles are measured clockwise or counterclockwise.

Experiment and note what happens to the coordinate display at the top of your screen (or the bottom in R13Win) as you select different UNITS modes. While you are at it, issue any or all of the inquiry commands and watch what happens. Do some dimensioning, too.

You should immediately note a significant fact: AutoCAD always works to about 14 digits, regardless of the UNITS setting. Any rounding off to suit the UNITS settings takes place only at the last instant, as inquiry values are displayed; however, the underlying database values are *not* altered. If you flip from eight-place decimals to ½-inch fractions and back, all the original decimal values will return unscathed.

To avoid apparent discrepancies, you should have your SNAP and GRID increments set to match the type of UNITS setting you are using. They should be an exact multiple or increment of your smallest unit; a SNAP setting of .100 is appropriate for three-place decimals but will give strange results with ¹⁄₁₆-inch (.0625) fractions.

Note also that the selected format affects *all* display actions and inquiry commands. It also affects the format of any dimensioning that you do *after* you change format and/or precision.

Data Entry Formats

When entering values from the keyboard, you can always reply with integers, decimals, scientific, or fractional formats, regardless of the current format set by UNITS. In addition, when architectural or engineering formats are active, you can also enter values in foot-and-inch format; for example, 15½ inches can be entered as 15.5, 1.55E+1, 15-½, 1'3-½", or 1'3.5". Note that there cannot be any spaces, because AutoCAD would act on them as it would an Enter, and that the foot (') and inch (") marks are required where shown.

You should now be able to see the connection between drawing scales, inquiry commands, and UNITS.

14 Customizing and System Management

In the preceding chapters I covered the fundamentals of the major AutoCAD two-dimensional drawing commands and operations. In this, the final chapter, I let you in on the secrets that separate the great AutoCAD users from the good ones.

Customizing

Most PC programs seem to be labeled "no user-serviceable parts inside," but not AutoCAD. One of AutoCAD's greatest strengths is the fact that it can be easily customized to suit your specific needs.

The Prototype Drawing

By default, whenever you start a *new* drawing AutoCAD actually starts by copying an *existing* drawing—a prototype—and bringing up that copy for you to add to and edit. The name and location of this default prototype drawing varies slightly with the version.

> **R12DOS:** The drawing is called ACAD, and it normally resides in the directory C:\ACAD\SUPPORT.

> **R12Win:** The drawing is called ACAD, and it normally resides in the directory C:\ACADWIN\SUPPORT.

R13DOS, R13Win: The drawing is called ACAD, and it normally resides in the directory C:\ACADR13\COMMON\ SUPPORT.

LT: The drawing is called ACLT, and it normally resides in the directory C:\ACLTWIN.

Whatever it is called, the prototype drawing is a drawing just like any other. The simplest way to start customizing AutoCAD is through this drawing. Simply bring it up for editing and then issue any commands you want; for example, the following:

▶ UNITS
Set to feet/inches, decimal, places of decimal, angle mode, and so on.

▶ LAYER
Create standard layer names, colors, and line types. For example, you can create a hidden layer, a center layer, and so on with the appropriate line types. It is also a good idea to create separate layers for text and dimensions. If you create a construction layer, when the drawing is complete you can freeze all other layers except that layer and then use ERASE Window to clean out all construction lines in one easy hit.

▶ LTSCALE
Set to match your most common plotting scale.

▶ DIMSCALE
Set to suit your common plotting scale.

▶ STYLE
Create standard text styles and sizes, taking into account your scale factor.

▶ LIMITS
Set to suit your most common drawing size, again taking into account the scale.

In addition, SNAP, GRID, ORTHO, BLIPMODE, and so on, can be set as your fancy moves you. You are not limited to settings. You can define standard detail blocks and draw a standard title block, your company logo, and standard notes—whatever you want.

When you are done, just save this drawing. Thereafter when you start a new drawing, AutoCAD will start it from a copy of your prototype drawing, and everything will be preset to your liking.

There are two major advantages to using a customized prototype drawing:

1. You save a lot of work each time you start a drawing.

2. The practice fosters uniformity between drawings, even when they are produced by different operators.

In particular, it is highly desirable that all workstations in a multiple-station office use the same prototype drawing. Doing this makes it much easier for anyone in the office to read or edit anyone else's drawings, because the format of all the drawings are consistent. Also, plotting will be easier, because AutoCAD selects plotter pens according to the colors. If everyone uses the same layers and hence the same colors, you won't have to change pens for each drawing.

Setting preferences in the prototype drawing is by far the most cost-effective way of customizing AutoCAD: 20 minutes spent modifying the prototype is 20 minutes saved *in every drawing you ever do from now on.*

Variable prototypes If you regularly use several different drawing sizes and/or scales, no problem: AutoCAD lets you override the default prototype drawing very simply. Just create several new drawings and give them the characteristics you want, along with suitable names. For example, you might have four, with limits set and borders drawn for A-size, B-size, C-size, and D-size paper. Save each of them. To work with this feature, follow these steps:

1. Start a new drawing. A dialog box appears, in which you usually enter the name of the new drawing (in the space near the bottom of the box). Note, however, the button near the top labeled "Prototype . . ." Beside the button is a space containing the name of the standard prototype drawing: ACLTWIN for LT, ACAD for all other versions. This is the default.

2. Either click on the space and type in the name of the draw-ing you want to be the prototype for the new drawing, or pick {Prototype . . .}. The standard file-selection dialog box appears. Scroll through the list of prototype file names in the usual manner and select a drawing.

3. Pick {OK}. AutoCAD starts a new drawing that is a copy of the desired prototype. The prototype is not altered.

Any existing drawing can be invoked as a prototype. A consul-tant could have a prototype for each client or for each project, while an architect could have one prototype for foundations, one for walls, and one for plumbing, each with a suitable title block, border, standard notes, and so on. If you are drawing something similar to an existing drawing, simply invoke the existing draw-ing as the prototype for the new one and make your changes. The original will not be altered.

No prototype What if you mess up the standard prototype draw-ing and want to start over? Or what if you want to start a new drawing that is *not* a copy of ACAD or any other prototype? No problem, just follow these steps:

1. Start a new drawing.

2. Enter the new drawing name (or the existing prototype drawing name).

3. Pick {No prototype}.

4. Pick {OK}. A new drawing is created with all its settings set to the AutoCAD defaults.

PREFERENCES

R12Win, LT, and R13Win allow you to set such things as whether the toolbox is on or off, the number of command lines visible at the bottom, the colors for the various portions of the editing screen, and so on.

> **R12Win and LT:** Pick {FILES} {PREFERENCES} to bring up a dialog box in which you make your changes. Note that in R12WIN you also must pick {Save to ACAD.INI} to make the settings stick for future sessions.

R13Win: Pick {OPTIONS} {PREFERENCES} to bring up a dialog box in which you make your changes.

R12DOS and R13DOS: These versions have no equivalent function.

Custom menus As explained in the AutoCAD manuals, the entire menu structure is not inherently built-in as a permanent feature of AutoCAD. Instead it is contained in a separate menu file that can be edited via any text editor or word processor. The commands appear in the menu file in plain English, just as you would type them at the keyboard. There are a few little hooks to watch out for when you edit the menu file, but you can't do any real damage. Just be sure to make a copy of the original before you start any editing session, so you can always revert to it if needed.

The screen menu, the tablet menu, and the mouse or digitizer buttons can all be customized. You can control what appears in the screen menu area, in the pull-down menus, and even in the icon menus.

Menu customizing is very useful if you find yourself using the same sequence of commands repeatedly. For example, you can set it so that whenever you pick TEXT, AutoCAD will automatically change to your TEXT layer first. Similarly, you could have a Hidden Line menu pick that changes to Hidden Layer and invokes LINE, or several Scale picks that automatically set the limits, ltscale, dimscale, and text style sizes.

You can also speed up menu loading and operation by weeding out unused commands from the standard menu. For example, if you are using a mouse you can delete the menu sections that start ***TABLET1, ***TABLET2, and so on. This will cut the file size in half.

AutoLISP AutoCAD (except LT) contains a built-in programming language based on LISP, which is used extensively in robotics and artificial intelligence. AutoLISP is a little weird in places, especially if you were raised on a normal language such as BASIC, but it is very powerful when dealing with the type of data required by AutoCAD. It supports the usual IF-THEN, WHILE, file handling, printing, and other features of most higher-level languages, but it also supports many graphics and database functions unique to AutoCAD.

You can use AutoLISP to build very complex routines in parametric design. AutoCAD can be set up to ask you a few questions such as size, type, speed, and load, and it will then generate a detailed drawing based on your replies.

Dialog boxes AutoCAD's Dialog Control Language (available in R12DOS, R12Win, R13DOS, R13DOS, and R13Win only) operates in conjunction with AutoLISP to allow you to create your own dialog boxes.

Recorder R12Win, LT, and R13Win are true Windows applications, so you can use the standard Windows RECORDER program to record individual keystrokes. They will then play back and drive AutoCAD when you hit the appropriate single "hot key," just as if you had typed in everything again at the Command prompt.

The bottom line is that the power and convenience of AutoCAD is limited only by your imagination. Using it as it comes out of the box is a lot like driving a car with four flat tires: it may beat walking all to blazes, but you could be doing an awful lot better.

System Management

Here are a few little tricks that will help you be more productive with AutoCAD.

Backups

The three most important factors in running a good computer installation are BACKUP, BACKUP, and BACKUP. That's right; computers crash or get stolen, buildings burn down, files get erased accidentally (or deliberately), and viruses *do* exist. At any given time, you should have *at least* three copies of your drawings, as follows:

▶   The current one in progress in your computer

▶   One on a separate floppy disk

▶ Another in a different building, even if you just take it home at night

A high-speed tape backup unit is almost mandatory for any good computer system and is very reasonably priced these days.

AutoCAD has an automatic timed backup facility, which will automatically save your drawing at a specified interval to a file called AUTO.SV$ in the current directory. However, before AutoCAD can open that file after a crash, you must go to DOS or the Windows File Manager and rename that file to something with the extension .DWG.

The interval between saves can be adjusted as follows:

> **R12DOS, R12Win, R13DOS, and R13Win:** From the Command prompt, type in the SAVETIME, then enter the desired interval, in minutes, between saves.

> **LT:** The safety interval is one of the settings in the PREFERENCES dialog box.

Working Directories

A small directory is a happy one. Most AutoCAD workstations seem to be set up so that all your drawings end up in the same subdirectory as the AutoCAD program, support, and sample files. This makes it very hard for you, and DOS, to find a specific file.

You should keep all your drawings in a separate directory or a series of subdirectories. This makes DOS and AutoCAD run faster and backups much simpler.

Here is another customizing trick: Recall from earlier in this chapter that when AutoCAD starts a new drawing, it copies the prototype drawing ACAD (ACLT in LT). AutoCAD looks for the drawing file in the *current* directory first. If it doesn't find it there, it then looks in the ..\SUPPORT directory and if necessary in the directory in which the AutoCAD program resides.

You thus can have different directories for each project, or each client, or each discipline, and each can have a different prototype drawing. You can ensure the appropriate prototype is used simply by changing to that directory before you start AutoCAD.

Doing this is made easy in R12Win, LT, and R13Win. You can create several Windows icons for AutoCAD, each with a distinct title and a suitable working directory. Then simply launch AutoCAD by clicking on the appropriate icon.

Conclusion

Having finished this book, you should have a pretty good understanding of AutoCAD fundamentals. With a little practice you should be able to efficiently produce two-dimensional drawings. If you want to proceed further with AutoCAD, the possibilities are almost limitless, including more customizing, working in 3D, and solid modeling. You can even branch into other AutoDesk products to get into shaded rendering and animation of your AutoCAD drawings.

As I said at the beginning, this book is not a replacement for the full AutoCAD manuals. There is a wealth of information tucked away in them.

You can also subscribe to one or more independent CAD magazines, such as *CADalyst, CADENCE,* and *AutoCAD User.* These contain many helpful hints from fellow users. They also keep you up to date on new AutoCAD releases, third-party add-in products, and hardware.

Also, join a local user group; there are always experienced users available to help beginners. And if you have a modem, you can subscribe to Compuserve and join GO ACAD, a forum directly supported by AutoCAD. You will often find that your questions are answered by the programmer who actually wrote that portion of AutoCAD.

Enjoy!

Index

Index

Index

Index